Paint Techniques
for Home Decorating
Walls, Furniture & Floors

Paint Techniques
for Home Decorating
Walls, Furniture & Floors

Sterling Publishing Co., Inc. New York

A Sterling / Chapelle Book

Chapelle:
- Jo Packham, Owner
- Cathy Sexton, Editor
- Staff: Areta Bingham, Malissa Boatwright, Kass Burchett, Rebecca Christensen, Marilyn Goff, Shirley Heslop, Holly Hollingsworth, Susan Jorgensen, Leslie Liechty, Pauline Locke, Ginger Mikkelsen, Barbara Milburn, Linda Orton, Karmen Quinney, Rhonda Rainey, Leslie Ridenour, and Cindy Stoeckl

If you have any questions or comments or would like information on specialty products featured in this book, please contact Chapelle, Ltd., Inc., P.O. Box 9252, Ogden, UT 84409 • (801) 621-2777 • (801) 621-2788 Fax

The written instructions, photographs, designs, patterns, and projects in this volume are intended for the personal use of the reader and may be reproduced for that purpose only. Any other use, especially commercial use, is forbidden under law without the written permission of the copyright holder. Every effort has been made to ensure that all the information in this book is accurate. However, due to differing conditions, tools, and individual skills, the publisher cannot be responsible for any injuries, losses, and other damages which may result from the use of the information in this book.

Due to the limited amount of space available, we must print our patterns at a reduced size in order to give our patrons the maximum number of patterns possible in our publications. We believe the quality and quantity of our patterns will compensate for any inconvenience this may cause.

Library of Congress Cataloging-in-Publication Data

Paint techniques for home decorating : walls, furniture & floors / Plaid.
        p.   cm.
     "A Sterling / Chapelle book."
     Includes index.
     ISBN 0-8069-0551-4
      1. Texture painting--Amateurs' manuals. 2. House painting--Amateurs' manuals.
  3. Furniture painting--Amateurs' manuals.
  I. Plaid Enterprises.
  TT323.P347 1997
  698'.1--dc21   97-35572
                            CIP

10 9 8 7 6 5 4 3 2 1

Published by Sterling Publishing Company, Inc.
387 Park Avenue South, New York, NY 10016
© 1998 by Chapelle Ltd.
Distributed in Canada by Sterling Publishing
c/o Canadian Manda Group, One Atlantic Avenue, Suite 105
Toronto, Ontario, Canada M6K 3E7
Distributed in Great Britain and Europe by Cassell PLC
Wellington House, 125 Strand, London WC2R 0BB, England
Distributed in Australia by Capricorn Link (Australia) Pty Ltd.
P.O. Box 6651, Baulkham Hills, Business Centre, NSW 2153, Australia
Printed and Bound in China
All Rights Reserved

Sterling ISBN 0-8069-0551-4

Contents

Contents

Introduction

We all want homes that are warm, welcoming, and wonderful to live in — homes that express our personality, celebrate our individuality, and showcase our creativity. Thanks to the wide variety of products that are now available to home decorators, it's never been easier to have the beautiful home you've always wanted.

This book contains a collection of do-it-yourself home decor projects created by talented and experienced designers. It shows you, step-by-step, how to create a variety of textures including sponging, ragging, mopping, brush texturing, and combing to enhance your walls and furniture. You'll also learn how to apply motifs to walls, furniture, and floors with techniques such as stenciling and block printing. You'll see ways to use pickling and antiquing to create the look of age and wear and discover clever tricks for using wallpaper. There are more than 45 projects, plus patterns and instructions for cutting your own stencils and printing blocks.

This book, with how-to information on all the techniques presented and lots of beautiful photographs, is a valuable reference you'll look to again and again. You'll also learn about the types of products (mostly waterbase, quick drying, and non-toxic) used to create these projects — products that are available at hardware, crafts, and building supply stores.

SURFACE PREPARATION

Cleaning the Wall(s):
Remove any soil or grease by washing the wall with rubbing alcohol, soapy water, or a commercial cleaner designed for use before painting. If using alcohol or soapy water, rinse thoroughly and let dry. If using a commercial cleaner, follow manufacturer's directions.

Repairing the Wall(s):
Repair any cracks or holes with spackling compound or dry wall joint compound, following package directions. Let dry. Sand smooth.

Use a sanding block or a small electric finishing sander for easier sanding on flat surfaces. You can make a sanding block by cutting a 3" long piece from a 2 x 4 and wrapping a piece of sandpaper around it. You can tape the sandpaper to hold it in place or you can hold it in place while you sand.

Sanding New Wood Furniture:
Sand new wood furniture with either 220 or 120 grit sandpaper, rubbing with the grain of the wood, to remove rough edges and smooth rough areas. Start with a coarser grit paper, then finish sanding with a finer grit.

- To round sharp edges for a worn look, use the coarse sandpaper to knock down the sharp corners. Finish with a fine grade.

- Smooth flat surfaces to prepare them for painting or staining. Often just a light sanding with 220 sandpaper is all that's needed. If the wood is very rough, start with a coarser grit paper, then move to a finer one.

- On some new, unfinished furniture, the factory may have allowed a small amount of glue to seep out from the joints. It is important to remove this dried glue, if the furniture is to be stained or finished with any transparent color, or the area will not accept the stain or wash. Sand away the glue, if possible. If sanding does not remove it all, scrape it lightly with a putty knife or a single edge razor blade.

- When sanding between coats of primer, paint, or varnish, always check the surface for smoothness. A true sign of a good job is that it feels smooth. If the surface appears to be scratched after sanding, you are using sandpaper or steel wool that's too coarse or you are sanding the surface before the paint, primer, or varnish is completely dry. Use a finer grit paper and/or let the surface dry completely and sand again.

Using a Tack Cloth:

Wipe away all dust after sanding with a tack cloth or a dry dust cloth. (A damp cloth would raise the grain of the wood.) To remove dust from crevices and corners, use a bristle brush, vacuum, or blow on the area.

Painted, Stained, or Varnished
Wood to Be Painted:

Dull the finish so the new paint will adhere properly.

- If paint or varnish is chipped, crackled, or crazed, sand smooth, following sanding instructions. Wipe away dust.

- If surface is soiled but the finish is intact, clean with a generous amount of rubbing alcohol to strip oils or soil from surface. Use a cloth or steel wool and rub with the grain of the wood. Rub each area smooth and dry before moving to another. Lightly sand any rough areas. Wipe away all dust.

- If paint buildup is heavy, chemical stripping may be necessary.

Painted or Varnished
Wood to Be Stained:

Strip paint or varnish, using a chemical stripper. Follow manufacturer's directions for the stripper you are using. Use a paint scraper to remove the paint, varnish, or waste and use newspapers to soak up this waste. Work with the grain of the wood. After most of the paint has been removed, rub the surface with coarse steel wool to remove more of the finish (again, working with the grain of wood). Use a ceramic cleaning tool to scrape away paint from tight or carved areas. When the surface is dry, sand smooth and wipe away dust.

You may also have a professional strip the project, if desired. Sometimes it costs less to get someone to do it than buying the products and equipment needed to do it yourself.

If you're going to apply antiquing, glazing, or a color wash, use sandpaper or steel wool to prepare the surface. Work in long smooth strokes, because the antiquing or color wash will pick up the direction of the sanding pattern and will show after it dries.

Using Primer:

- If the furniture is NOT going to be stained, apply a coat of white spray primer. Let dry. The primer seals the wood and prevents any dark areas of wood from showing through a light colored basecoat. It also prevents any knot holes from bleeding through months later. You should not be able to see the dark areas or knot holes after priming. If you do, apply another coat of primer in these areas.

- DO NOT USE PRIMER if your project is to be stained, glazed, pickled, or given a painted faux finish which involves distressing after painting. (A distressed finish is scraped and sanded in places down through the paint to give an aged look, and the white primer would show, ruining the effect.) After the primer is dry, sand the surface with 220 grit sandpaper, sanding with the grain of the wood. Wipe away dust.

- Many times it is not necessary to completely strip a piece of furniture — just get it smooth and remove most of the varnish. In this case, sand first with a fine grade of sandpaper or steel wool.

- If you have a piece of furniture that has been painted with oil-base paint or with layers of old paint, you do not have to strip this piece to be able to paint on another layer of paint. Use 120 grit sandpaper until the surface appears dusty and smooth, then use 220 sandpaper to smooth the surface.

- When sanding an old painted surface, you must change the sandpaper often due to paint buildup that occurs on the paper.

Filling Holes:

If there are nail holes, cracks, or gaps where sections of the wood meet, fill these in with a neutral color stainable latex filler. Apply as little as possible to fill the problem area, using your finger or a very small palette knife. Remove any excess while wet. Let dry, then sand smooth. If the area appears sunken after drying (sometimes the filler shrinks as it dries), repeat with a second application to level it out. Sand again when dry.

Applying Basecoat:

The basecoat is the first coat of the base color. Apply it by brushing the paint in the direction of the wood grain. Let dry. Sand the surface with 220 grit sandpaper, sanding with the grain of the wood. Wipe away all dust. Apply the second coat of the base color and let dry. If a third coat of paint is needed, sand and wipe away dust as before.

Sanding between coats of paint smoothes the raised wood grain and gives the surface better tooth for the next coat of paint.

Finishing:

Choose sealers that are non-yellowing and quick drying. Aerosol sealers are convenient and are available in gloss or matte finishes.

After the finish coats are applied and dry, if you think the project is too "shiny" (even though you used a matte finish), buff it with a fine grade of steel wool or water-moistened 400 grit sandpaper. This will remove any shine and give a buffed look.

- On painted surfaces, spray the dry, completed project with a coat of sealer. Let dry. Spray a second coat and let dry. Sand the surface with 400 grit sandpaper (it will be less abrasive if you wet it) or with a fine grade of steel wool. Wipe away all dust. If needed, apply a third finish coat or more.

- If the project is made of new wood and was stained or glazed, keep in mind that the wood has never been sealed and is rather porous. This means the surface will soak up most of the first coat of finish. It will, therefore, require more coats than a painted surface.

- A piece that will receive a lot of use will need more finish coats for protection. If your project is to be used outdoors or is a surface such as a table top that will receive heavy use, apply a protective sealer such as a polyurethane. Both matte and gloss finishes are appropriate. Apply according to manufacturer's directions.

- Applying only one or two coats of finish on a distressed surface will keep it looking weathered, worn, and aged.

Designers

Plaid® Enterprises
Publication Staff:

Mickey Baskett, Editor

Phyllis Mueller, Copy Editor

Susan Mickey, Stylist

Jeff Herr, Photographer

Suzanne Yoder,
Product Manager

Plaid® Enterprises
Designing Staff:

Susan Goans Driggers has made a fascinating career of her love of art and painting.

Jane Gauss began teaching stenciling after years teaching accounting and economics.

Liza Glenn learned how to block print while decorating a summer cottage and soon left her successful catering business to enjoy a lifelong interest in painting and decorative arts.

Kathi Malarchuk left corporate America to pursue her love of art and design as a career.

Jackie Wynia's love of crafting has lead her to a career in both the needlework and crafts fields. Because of her expertise in several areas of crafts, she is able to pull together a variety of craft techniques to create entire design programs for manufacturers.

Sponging Techniques

Cellulose sponge texture

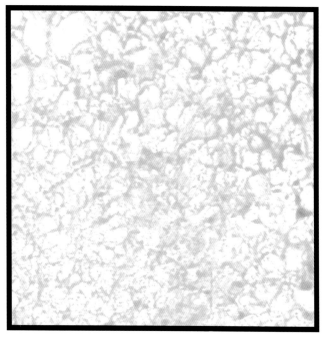

Sea sponge texture

Sponging can produce subtle color variation to walls and furniture, adding interest and texture to surfaces. It is probably one of the easiest surface finishes to achieve, yet there are many ways to do the technique.

Shown in this chapter are some of the easiest and most effective sponging techniques, such as all-over sponging, as well as how to create a checkerboard effect with a square sponge.

One Color Sponging:

Start with a light colored wall and sponge with a light or medium shade of glaze. The glaze color should be darker than the color of the wall. Adding this sponging texture instantly moves the wall from boring to exciting. It is also possible to start with a dark colored wall and sponge with a light color on top. It will be a very different look, but quite effective.

Two Color Sponging:

To add greater depth to your wall texture, sponge with a dark or medium shade of glaze. Next, sponge over the top with a lighter shade.

TIPS:

- "Pounce" the sponge onto the surface. Do not rub or drag the sponge. You will get a more defined sponge image this way.

- Do not overwork the surface. Don't keep pouncing the sponge in the same place. Pounce once and move on, slightly overlapping each application. The desired effect is to have some of the underneath wall color showing through.

- When sponging, do not keep the sponge in the same position. Move it around so the pattern is not the same each time you hit the surface.

SUPPLIES YOU WILL NEED

Paint:

The type of paint used for sponging should be slightly transparent and have a longer drying time than regular acrylic paint. This can be achieved by mixing an acrylic paint with a glazing medium or paint conditioner. A variety of acrylic paint types can be mixed with the glazing medium: acrylic craft paint, latex wall paint, and colored glaze. Ratios for mixing should follow the manufacturer's directions. Pre-mixed sponging paints can also be used.

Tools:

Sponges and sponge mitts can be used.

Sponge mitts make it very convenient to sponge without messy hands. These sponges and sponge mitts are available at hardware and craft stores.

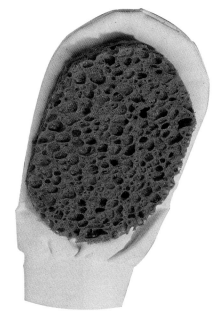

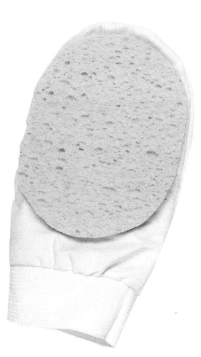

Sea sponge or cellulose sponge: If using a cellulose sponge, tear portions from the straight edges to make them more ragged so when you sponge, the result will not be a straight line image. Also, tear little bits out of the surface of the sponge to make it a little less uniform in texture.

Sea sponge mitt: A sea sponge texture is attached to a fabric mitt.

Cellulose sponge mitt: A cellulose sponge texture is attached to a fabric mitt. No tearing is necessary.

1 Prepare and paint surface. Let dry. Pour the acrylic craft paint, latex wall paint, or colored glaze into the glazing medium or paint conditioner and mix thoroughly. The amount of paint needed will depend on the depth of color you desire; more paint will give a darker color. Adding the paint to the glazing medium will result in a slightly transparent paint that has a longer drying time, therefore allowing you more time to do the sponging.

2 Always begin with a damp sponge. Dip the sponge into water, then squeeze out as much water as possible. Pour the glaze mixture onto a disposable plate. Dip the sponge into the glaze mixture to load paint onto the sponge. After loading the sponge, blot the surface of the sponge onto a clean disposable plate to distribute the paint. When it is necessary for excess paint to be removed from the sponge, blot the surface of the sponge on a paper towel or scrap piece of paper.

3 "Pounce" the sponge onto the surface. Move the sponge over the surface, pouncing and slightly overlapping each application.

A sea sponge will give excellent results when sponging walls and furniture.

French Country Kitchen

Pictured on page 13.

Designed by
Susan Goans Driggers

This cheery kitchen has sponged walls and a simple freehand border created with paint crayons. When the crayon cures, it won't rub off or smudge. For extra protection in an area that receives heavy use, apply a protective finish after the crayon has cured.

GATHER THESE SUPPLIES

Paint:
Latex wall paint,
    flat finish: white
Glazing medium: neutral
Colored glaze: plate blue
Paint crayon: blue chintz

Tools:
Sea sponge or
    sea sponge mitt
Ruler and pencil

Other Supplies:
Masking tape

INSTRUCTIONS

Prepare:

1. Prepare walls. See "Surface Preparation," pages 7-9.

2. Paint walls with white latex wall paint. Let dry.

3. Tape around molding and cabinets to protect them from sponging.

4. Determine how wide you want your top border to be and measure and mark from ceiling or ceiling molding.

(The border shown is 9". You can adjust the width to fit your room.) Tape above marks.

Sponge the Walls:

1. Mix plate blue glaze with glazing medium to desired shade.

2. Sponge walls with glaze mixture. Let dry. Remove tape.

Create the Border:

1. Prepare paint crayon by rubbing the tip on a paper towel to remove the hard coating.

2. Using the photo on page 13 as a guide, or using your own design, lightly mark design in unsponged area just below ceiling or ceiling molding with a pencil.

3. Mark over pencil lines with blue chintz paint crayon to complete border design.

Checkerboard Table

Pictured on page 15.

Designed by
Susan Goans Driggers

An ordinary cellulose sponge was used to stamp the checkerboard design on the table top and to add texture and interest to the edges and the apron. The design idea can be used on any square surface.

GATHER THESE SUPPLIES

Square wooden table

Paint:
Latex wall paint,
    flat finish: white
Glazing medium: neutral
Acrylic craft paint: terra-cotta

Tools:
Cellulose sponge
Ruler and pencil

Other Supplies:
Matte spray sealer

INSTRUCTIONS

Prepare:

1. Prepare table. See "Surface Preparation," pages 7-9.

2. Paint table with two or three coats of white latex wall paint. Let dry and sand between coats.

3. Cut the cellulose sponge into a square. The size of the square is determined by the size of the table. This table top is 16½" square. To achieve six rows of squares, the sponge was cut into a 2¾" square (2¾" X 6 = 16½").

4. Lightly mark design on table top with a pencil.

Sponge the Checks:

1. Mix terra-cotta acrylic craft paint with glazing medium to create a dark terra-cotta shade. You will only need a small amount of glaze mixture when doing a small table — about one cup is enough.

2. Load square sponge with glaze mixture. Blot sponge on a scrap piece of paper to remove excess paint and to see how much pressure is needed to stamp the square shape.

3. Press sponge on table top to create the checkerboard pattern. Let dry. To achieve a darker color, sponge squares a second time. Let dry.

Antique and Trim:

1. Antique the table with the glaze mixture, working one section at a time. To do this, dip the same sponge into the glaze mixture. Rub a light coat over the entire table top. Rinse the sponge, then squeeze out as much water as possible.

2. Pat the sponge over the glaze mixture while it is still wet. This will result in a very pale shade.

3. Repeat to antique the apron and legs, working one section at a time.

4. Sponge edges of table top, bottom edges of apron, and tips of legs two or more times to add more color to these areas. Let dry.

Finish:

1. Spray with matte sealer.

Provincial Kitchen

Pictured on page 17.

Designed by
Susan Goans Driggers

Sponging, stippling, and stenciling techniques were combined to create the rustic look on this kitchen wall. The upper portion of the wall is sponged and stippled. The faux tile pattern on the lower portion of the wall is sponged and stenciled. The painted border that divides the two areas was masked off with tape and heavily sponged.

GATHER THESE SUPPLIES

Paint:
Latex wall paint,
 flat finish: pale green
Glazing medium: neutral
Colored glaze: moss green
Acrylic craft paint:
 earthenware

Tools:
Sea sponge or
 sea sponge mitt
Stippling brush
Ruler and pencil
Plumb line
Craft knife

Other Supplies:
Masking tape
Stencil blank material

INSTRUCTIONS

Prepare:

1. Prepare wall. See "Surface Preparation," pages 7-9.

2. Paint wall with pale green latex wall paint. Let dry.

3. Draw two parallel horizontal lines on the wall with a pencil to make a narrow border between the upper and lower portions of the wall. Tape below the upper line.

Sponge and Stipple the Upper Wall:

1. Mix moss green glaze with glazing medium to desired tint.

2. Sponge wall above taped line with glaze mixture. Let dry.

3. Using a stippling brush, stipple wall over the sponged surface to create a textured look. Let dry. Remove tape. Reserve remaining glaze mixture.

Sponge and Stencil the Lower Wall:

1. Draw a diamond the size you want the "tile" to be. Using stencil blank material and a craft knife, cut diamond-shaped stencil according to manufacturer's directions.

2. Tape above the lower line. Using a plumb line, make a vertical line on the wall to mark the placement of the first diamond.

3. Position diamond-shaped stencil on wall, using marked plumb line as a guide. Sponge opening of stencil with earthenware acrylic craft paint, sponging edges more heavily than centers. See photo on page 17. Complete all diamond shapes, leaving a small amount of space between them for grout lines. Let dry. Don't worry if the lines and diamonds aren't perfectly straight.

4. Sponge centers of diamonds and along some edges with reserved moss green glaze mixture. Let dry. Remove tape.

Sponge the Border:

1. Tape above the upper line of the border and below the lower line of the border.

2. Solidly sponge the border with earthenware acrylic craft paint. Let dry 30 minutes. Remove tape. Let dry thoroughly.

Ragging Techniques

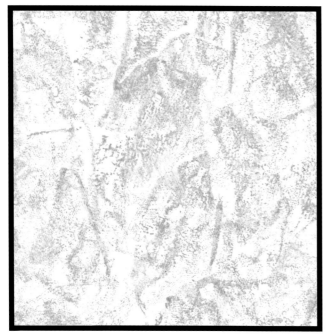

Patina glaze ragged on a white wall

Roseberry glaze ragged on a white wall

Ragging gives random texture and color to surfaces and is a great way to disguise minor flaws in plaster and drywall. It is called ragging because cloth rags are used to create the texture. A colored glaze mixture is applied over a painted surface, using rolls of rags or a ragging mitt. The effect can be dramatic or subtle, depending on the amount of contrast in the colors used and the intensity of the colors themselves.

Shown in this chapter are a range of possibilities, including ragged stripes for living room walls, ragging with metallic paint for a dramatic effect in a bathroom, and ragging on furniture.

Ragging With More Than One Color:

When ragging with more than one color, repeat the procedure with subsequent colors. Use a clean ragging mitt or rag and a clean disposable bowl for each paint color.

Negative Ragging Method:

Brush glaze mixture onto a painted surface that is thoroughly dry. Moisten a clean ragging mitt or rag and pat over wet paint, removing paint to create the ragged texture.

TIPS:

• For more defined texture, don't rub or drag the ragging mitt or crumpled rags. By rubbing you will get a blurred image. Instead, "pounce" the surface.

• Do not overwork the surface by ragging in the same area repeatedly. You want the texture to be distinct.

• Overlap the ragging so there is not a noticeable beginning and ending.

• If a more subtle look is desired, your wall paint color and your glaze mixture color should be close to the same color.

• For more contrast and drama on your walls or furniture, your wall paint color and your glaze mixture color should highly contrast with one another.

SUPPLIES YOU WILL NEED

Paint:

The type of paint used for ragging should be slightly transparent and have a longer drying time than regular acrylic paint. This can be achieved by mixing an acrylic paint with a glazing medium or paint conditioner. A variety of acrylic paint types can be mixed with the glazing medium: acrylic craft paint, latex wall paint, and colored glaze. Ratios for mixing should follow the manufacturer's directions. Pre-mixed sponging paints can also be used.

Tools:

Rags and ragging mitts can be used.

When using rags, cut strips about 10" x 20" from 100% cotton t-shirt fabric or cheesecloth. You will use these to roll along the surface as shown in the hands on photos.

Ragging mitts make it very convenient to create a ragged finish without messy hands. These ragging mitts are available at hardware and craft stores.

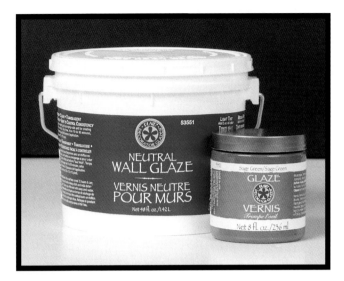

Two glaze colors ragged on a white wall in vertical stripes

*Ragging mitt:
Loops of fabric are attached to a cloth mitt.*

Using Rags

1 Prepare and paint surface. Let dry. Pour the acrylic craft paint, latex wall paint, or colored glaze into the glazing medium or paint conditioner and mix thoroughly. The amount of paint needed will depend on the depth of color you desire; more paint will give a darker color. Adding the paint to the glazing medium will result in a slightly transparent paint that has a longer drying time, therefore allowing you more time to do the ragging.

Always begin with a damp rag. Dip the rag into water, then squeeze out as much water as possible. Pour some of the glaze mixture into a disposable bowl. Wearing gloves, dip the rag into the glaze mixture to load paint onto the rag. Wring out by pulling the rag between your thumb and first finger. Wipe the glaze mixture from your hands.

2 Crumple the rag into a rosette and, using both hands, pat the rag onto the surface. Keep the rag crumpled and shaped — you don't want it to get too flat. Reload the rag with glaze mixture as needed.

3 Another way to use rags is to roll the rag into a loose tube shape and, using both hands, roll the rag tube over the wall. Change positions frequently to avoid a striped effect. This method is called "rag rolling."

4 Regardless of the application method being used, don't rub or drag the rags. By rubbing you will get a blurred image. Instead, "pounce" the surface to make certain the result is a more defined texture. Never overwork the surface as you want the texture to be distinct. Overlap the ragging so there is not a noticeable beginning and ending.

Using Ragging Mitts

1 Prepare and paint surface. Let dry. Pour the acrylic craft paint, latex wall paint, or colored glaze into the glazing medium or paint conditioner and mix thoroughly. The amount of paint needed will depend on the depth of color you desire; more paint will give a darker color. Adding the paint to the glazing medium will result in a slightly transparent paint that has a longer drying time, therefore allowing you more time to do the ragging.

2 Always begin with a damp mitt. Dip the face of the mitt into water, then squeeze out as much water as possible. Pour some of the glaze mixture onto a disposable plate. Wearing the mitt, dip the rag into the glaze mixture to load paint onto the rag. After loading the rag, blot the surface of the rag onto a clean disposable plate to distribute the paint.

3 Pat the rag onto the surface. Move the rag over the surface, patting and slightly overlapping each application. Change positions frequently and reload the rag with glaze mixture as needed.

Walls with Ragged Stripes

Pictured on page 23.

Designed by
Susan Goans Driggers

For this wall treatment, suitable for a variety of rooms, wide stripes are masked off on the walls with masking tape. Two colors of glaze are ragged to create subtle texture and color.

GATHER THESE SUPPLIES

Paint:
Latex wall paint,
   flat finish: white
Glazing medium: neutral
Colored glaze: linen white
   and tuscan sunset

Tools:
Rags or ragging mitt
Ruler and pencil
Plumb line

Other Supplies:
Masking tape

INSTRUCTIONS

Prepare:

1. Prepare walls. See "Surface Preparation," pages 7-9.

2. Paint walls with white latex wall paint. Let dry.

3. Using a plumb line, find and mark a straight vertical line on one wall. Never start in the corner, assuming it is straight — corners rarely are. Lightly mark the line with a pencil. Don't use a chalk line — it's too messy. Tape along the vertical line.

4. Measure 10" and place another vertical line of tape. Continue to measure 10" widths and tape along the vertical lines. Occasionally check the lines with the plumb line to make certain they are straight. Use the plumb line on both sides of corners. You may need to adjust the width of the stripe in the corners so the result is visually pleasing and the line does not fall too close to a corner.

Rag the Stripes:

1. Mix linen white glaze with glazing medium to desired shade.

2. Rag walls, inside every other taped stripe, with glaze mixture. Let dry. Remove tape.

3. Tape along the vertical lines so you can paint remaining stripes.

4. Mix tuscan sunset glaze with glazing medium to desired shade.

5. Rag remaining stripes on walls with glaze mixture. Let dry. Remove tape.

Ragged End Table

Pictured on page 23.

Designed by
Susan Goans Driggers

On this end table, a ragged finish gives a mottled texture. The use of a brown glaze mixture over a brown base coat creates subtle contrast.

GATHER THESE SUPPLIES

Drop leaf end table

Paint:
Glazing medium: neutral
Colored glaze: black and
   russet
Acrylic craft paint:
   buckskin brown

Tools:
Rags or ragging mitt

Other Supplies:
Matte spray sealer

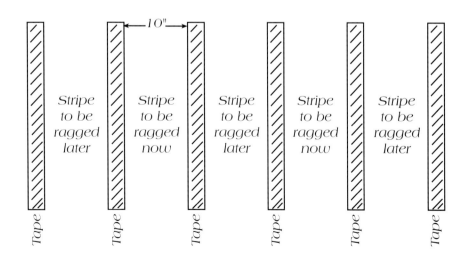

INSTRUCTIONS

Prepare:

1. Prepare table. See "Surface Preparation," pages 7-9.

2. Paint table with one or two coats of buckskin brown acrylic craft paint. Let dry and sand between coats.

Rag the Table:

1. Mix one-eighth part black glaze and one part russet glaze with two parts glazing medium.

2. Rag table, including drawers, drawer pulls, and legs, with glaze mixture. Let dry.

3. Spray with matte sealer.

Sponged Chest of Drawers

Pictured on page 25.

Designed by
Susan Goans Driggers

Three colors of glaze give this simple chest of drawers a wonderful textured look. The bronze color was also used to create a design on the top and was used on the drawer pulls.

See chapter on Sponging for more details on this technique.

GATHER THESE SUPPLIES

Chest of drawers

Paint:
Latex wall paint,
  flat finish: white
Glazing medium: neutral
Colored glaze: olde world
  bronze, penny copper,
  and red

Tools:
Sea sponge or
  sea sponge mitt
Foam brush, 2"
Ruler and pencil
Pencil compass
Craft knife

Other Supplies:
Masking tape
Matte spray sealer

INSTRUCTIONS

Prepare:

1. Remove drawer pulls.

2. Prepare chest of drawers. See "Surface Preparation," pages 7-9.

3. Paint chest of drawers with two coats of white latex wall paint. Let dry.

Sponge the Chest of Drawers:

1. Make three different glaze mixtures. Mix one part each of olde world bronze, penny copper, and red glaze with two parts glazing medium.

2. Sponge chest of drawers with red glaze mixture. Let dry and rinse sponge.

3. Sponge chest of drawers with penny copper glaze mixture. Let dry and rinse sponge.

4. Sponge chest of drawers with olde world bronze glaze mixture. Let dry.

Trim and Finish:

1. Using the photo on page 25 as a guide, tape off the borders on the top.

2. Tape off a 2" border along bottom edge of chest of drawers, following the shape of the chest. To do this, position masking tape along the line of the border. Using the pencil compass, draw the 2" border on the masking tape. Using a craft knife, cut the tape along the line. Remove the tape below the line.

3. Paint the top and bottom borders and the drawer pulls with olde world bronze glaze. Don't use the glaze mixture; use glaze that has not been mixed with glazing medium. Let dry 30 minutes. Remove tape. Let dry thoroughly.

4. Spray with matte sealer.

5. Replace drawer pulls.

Ragged Accent Table

Pictured on page 25.

Designed by
Susan Goans Driggers

This simple painted table is made special with a ragged finish. The ragging is applied over both the base and the

trim colors, using the negative method. The glaze mixture is brushed on and rags or a ragging mitt are pounced over the surface to remove the glaze and create the texture.

GATHER THESE SUPPLIES

Rectangular wooden table

Paint:
Latex wall paint,
  flat finish: pale yellow
Glazing medium: neutral
Colored glaze: russet brown
Acrylic craft paint: maroon

Tools:
Rags or ragging mitt
Foam brush, 2"

Other Supplies:
Masking tape
Matte spray sealer

INSTRUCTIONS

Prepare:

1. Prepare table. See "Surface Preparation," pages 7-9.

2. Paint table with two or three coats of pale yellow latex wall paint. Let dry and sand between coats.

3. Paint edges of table top with maroon acrylic craft paint. Let dry.

Rag the Table:

1. Mix one part russet brown glaze with two parts glazing medium.

2. Using a 2" foam brush, paint the glaze mixture on the legs. Pat the rags or ragging mitt over the glaze mixture while it is still wet, removing

glaze to create the ragged texture.

3. Repeat on the apron and the table top. Let dry.

4. Spray with matte sealer.

Ragged Kitchen

Pictured on page 27.

Designed by
Susan Goans Driggers

Ragging adds wonderful texture and color to the upper part of these kitchen walls. The mushroom color was chosen for the ragging to coordinate with the rustic furniture and flower prints.

GATHER THESE SUPPLIES

Paint:
Latex wall paint,
  flat finish:
    white and cranberry
Latex wall paint,
  semi-gloss: white
Glazing medium: neutral
Colored glaze: mushroom

Tools:
Rags or ragging mitt

Other Supplies:
Masking tape

INSTRUCTIONS

Prepare:

1. Prepare walls. See "Surface Preparation," pages 7-9.

2. Paint upper walls with white latex wall paint. Let dry.

3. Paint lower walls with cranberry latex wall paint. Let dry.

4. Paint chair rail with semi-gloss white latex wall paint. Let dry.

5. Tape around chair rail to protect it from ragging.

Rag the Walls:

1. Mix one part mushroom glaze with six parts glazing medium.

2. Rag walls with glaze mixture. Let dry. Remove tape.

Rag the Corners:

1. For color and texture consistency with the walls, rag the corners at the same time you rag the adjacent walls. Don't do all the corners first or last.

Option #1:
For best results, tape off a small section of the adjacent wall at the corner so you can press the face of the ragging mitt firmly and closely without smearing the adjacent wall. Let dry. Remove tape. Tape other side. Press ragging mitt in corner. Let dry. Remove tape carefully.

Option #2:
Place the ragging mitt at the corner. Use your free hand to press the face of the ragging mitt into the corner. Repeat until corner is complete.

Golden Bathroom

Pictured on page 29.

Designed by
Susan Goans Driggers

Ragging with a metallic glaze can add drama and elegance to walls. Here, gold metallic glaze was ragged over white walls. The walls provide a coordinated, pleasing background for the framed art and accessories.

GATHER THESE SUPPLIES

Paint:
Latex wall paint,
   flat finish: white or ivory
Glazing medium: neutral
Colored glaze: new gold leaf

Tools:
Rags or ragging mitt

Other Supplies:
Masking tape

INSTRUCTIONS

Prepare:

1. Prepare walls. See "Surface Preparation," pages 7-9.

2. Paint walls with white or ivory latex wall paint. Let dry.

3. Tape around molding and cabinets to protect them from ragging.

Rag the Walls:

1. Mix new gold leaf glaze with glazing medium to desired shade.

2. Rag walls with glaze mixture. Let dry. Remove tape.

TIPS FOR USING RAGGING MITTS ON WALLS:

- Use masking tape at the corner on the adjacent wall. Rag into the corner. Let dry. Remove tape. Tape the corner on the ragged wall. Rag the second wall. Let dry. See diagrams below.

- Start on a wall that will be less visible, such as the wall that is behind you when you walk in the room. This will help you establish your technique. By the time you get to the most visible walls, you will be a pro.

- When working with metallic glazes, make certain the lighting is good. Metallic glazes reflect light differently at different angles. Look at the wall from different angles as you work.

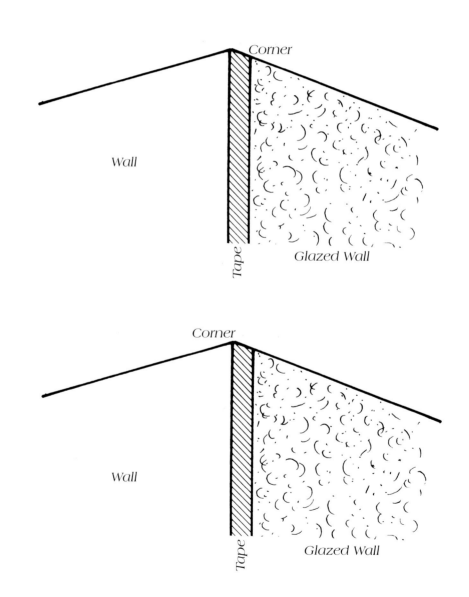

28

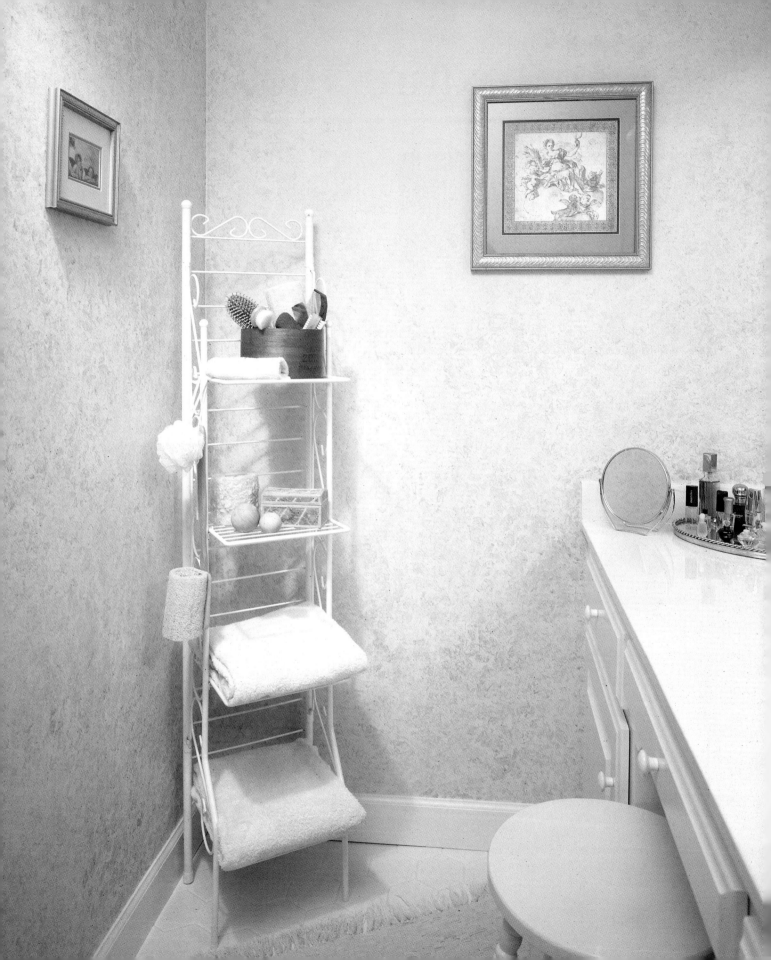

Brush Texture Techniques

A variety of textures can be created on surfaces with brushes. You can stipple combinations of colors or create brushed borders or overall patterns.

TYPES OF BRUSHES YOU CAN USE

French Brush:

The French brush is a natural bristle paint brush with short, fine bristles for creating faux finishes, patterns, and textures.

Stippling Brush:

A stippling brush is a palm-sized brush without a handle that has been designed especially for stippling. It is convenient to use and comfortable to hold.

Stiff Bristle Paint Brush:

You can also use a stiff bristle paint brush for stippling or brush strokes.

Pompeii red glaze stippled on a white wall with a French brush

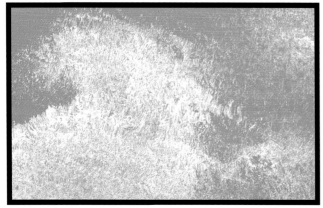

Clouds: Undiluted white glaze stippled on a medium blue wall

Basketweave: Undiluted patina glaze crisscrossed on a pale green wall

Using Positive Application with Glazing Medium

1 Prepare and paint surface. Let dry. Pour the acrylic craft paint, latex wall paint, or colored glaze into the glazing medium or paint conditioner and mix thoroughly. Pour a small amount of glaze mixture onto a disposable plate. Dip the tips of the brush bristles into the glaze mixture to load paint onto the brush.

2 Hold the brush perpendicular to the surface. "Pounce" the brush onto the surface, pressing the brush hard enough to force the bristles apart. Keep a rag or cloth nearby to periodically wipe the bristles. Reload the brush with glaze mixture as needed.

Using Positive Application with Water

1 Prepare and paint surface. Let dry. Pour one color of the acrylic craft paint, latex wall paint, or colored glaze into an equal amount of water and mix thoroughly. Pour a second color into an equal amount of water and mix thoroughly. Lightly mist surface after it is dry.

2 Using one brush for each color of diluted paint, randomly pounce the two paint colors over the surface, overlapping occasionally.

31

Using Negative Application

1 Prepare and paint surface. Let dry. Pour the acrylic craft paint, latex wall paint, or colored glaze into the glazing medium or paint conditioner and mix thoroughly. Pour a small amount of glaze mixture onto a disposable plate or into a paint roller pan. Dip a foam brush or paint roller into the glaze mixture to load paint onto the brush or roller. Paint entire wall, small sections at a time, with the glaze mixture.

2 Hold the brush or roller perpendicular to the surface. "Pounce" the brush onto the surface, over the wet glaze, to remove some of the glaze and create a texture. Lift the brush from the surface and rub the brush bristles over an old cloth to remove the glaze so bristles stay clean and dry. The temperature and amount of air circulation in the room will determine the drying time. The glaze mixture needs to be textured before it starts to dry.

Pastoral Bedroom

Pictured on page 33.

Designed by
Susan Goans Driggers

The walls of this restful retreat were brushed with coordinating glaze colors.

GATHER THESE SUPPLIES

Paint:
Latex wall paint,
    flat finish: mint green
Glazing medium: neutral
Colored glaze: russet brown
    and sage green

Tools:
Stippling brushes (2)

Other Supplies:
Masking tape

INSTRUCTIONS

Prepare:

1. Prepare walls. See "Surface Preparation," pages 7-9.

2. Paint walls with mint green latex wall paint. Let dry.

3. Tape around molding and cabinets to protect them from glazing.

Brush the Walls:

1. Mix russet brown glaze with half the glazing medium to make a dark shade.

2. Mix sage green glaze with the remaining glazing medium.

3. Apply the glaze mixture to the walls, using one of the options described at right. Work each color into and over the other, but don't work the surface so much that the glaze mixtures become one color — they should remain distinct colors. Let dry.

Option #1:
    Apply both colors at the same time, using one brush with one color glaze mixture in one hand and the other brush with the other color glaze mixture in your other hand.

Option #2:
    Apply the colors alternately, using one brush for each color, working your way around the room.

Option #3:
    Use the "buddy system" — you apply one color glaze mixture with one brush and have a buddy apply the other color glaze mixture with the other brush.

French Blue Bedroom

Pictured on page 35.

Designed by
Susan Goans Driggers

Above the chair rail, a stippled texture with high contrast is achieved by applying a glaze mixture with a French brush using the positive application method. Below the chair rail, the glaze mixture is applied to the wall and the brush is used to remove some of the glaze and create texture with less contrast using the negative application method. The same brush is used to brush the criss-cross basketweave design of the chair rail.

GATHER THESE SUPPLIES

Paint:
Latex wall paint,
  flat finish: pale blue
Glazing medium: neutral
Colored glaze: sky blue

Tools:
French brush
Foam brush or paint roller
Ruler and pencil

Other Supplies:
Masking tape

INSTRUCTIONS

Prepare:

1. Prepare walls. See "Surface Preparation," pages 7-9.

2. Paint walls with pale blue latex wall paint. Let dry.

3. Measure and mark two parallel horizontal lines to create the chair rail. Inside the lines, tape off the wide stripe.

Stipple the Upper Walls:

1. Mix one part sky blue glaze with six parts glazing medium.

2. Using the positive application with glazing medium, hold the brush perpendicular to the wall. "Pounce" the brush onto the walls, pressing the brush hard enough to force the bristles apart. Keep a rag or cloth nearby to periodically wipe the bristles. Reload the brush with glaze mixture as needed and continue until upper walls are covered.

Stipple the Lower Wall:

1. Using the negative application, apply the glaze mixture to the walls below the chair rail with a foam brush or paint roller. Hold the French brush perpendicular to the wall and pounce the bristles over the wet glaze. Lift the brush from the surface. Continue until lower walls have a soft texture. Let dry. Remove tape.

Brush the Chair Rail:

1. Tape above and below the chair rail area.

2. Tape angled stripes 1 1/2" wide in one direction along chair rail.

3. Dip stippling brush in glaze mixture. Brush each stripe, using the side of the brush and creating streaks with the glaze. Let dry. Remove tape.

4. Tape angled stripes 1 1/2" wide in the opposite direction along chair rail.

5. Brush each stripe as you did in step three. On every other stripe, when you get to a previously painted stripe, pick up the brush and place it on the other side of the painted stripe to achieve the woven effect. See photo on page 35. Let dry. Remove tape.

6. Tape off a narrow border above the chair rail and a wider border below the chair rail. Using long horizontal strokes, brush borders with glaze mixture. Let dry. Remove tape.

Splashed Stone Chest

Pictured on page 37.

Designed by
Susan Goans Driggers

Splashed stone is a wet-on-wet marbleizing technique that can render a faux stone finish on all kinds of surfaces. This chest has the splashed stone finish on the top, drawer fronts, feet, and trim. Gold trim accents the drawer fronts and drawer pulls.

GATHER THESE SUPPLIES

Wooden chest with
   three drawers

Paint:

Acrylic craft paint:
   warm white
Glazing medium: neutral
Colored glaze: new gold leaf,
   sage green, and soft teal

Tools:

Poly sponge brush, 2"
French brush
Eye dropper

Other Supplies:

Posterboard
Damp cloth
Rubbing alcohol
Masking tape
Matte spray sealer

INSTRUCTIONS

Prepare:

1. Remove drawer pulls.

2. Prepare wooden chest.
See "Surface Preparation,"
pages 7-9.

3. Paint wooden chest with
one to three coats of warm
white acrylic craft paint.
Let dry.

4. Using the photo on page
37 as a guide, tape around
areas to be finished with the
splashed stone technique to
protect all other areas from
splashed stone finish.

Creating the Splashed Stone Finish:

1. Test your technique on a
piece of posterboard before
you begin working on your
project surface. Experiment
until you get the results you
want. Work on one area at a
time so the glaze stays moist.
Whenever possible, turn the
project so you are working on
horizontal surfaces. If you
must work on a vertical
surface, it's best to keep the
paints a little drier, although
this will lessen the water-
splashed appearance.

2. Brush a coat of glazing
medium on surfaces that are
to receive the splashed stone
finish. Do not let dry!

3. While surface is moist, use
the tips of a French brush to
randomly pounce soft teal
glaze over the glazing medium. You should be able to
see the base coat color. Keep
the brush perpendicular to the
surface. Use a damp cloth to
wipe some of the colored
glaze from the bristles of the
brush before pouncing the
next color onto the project.

4. Repeat the procedure
using sage green glaze.

5. Apply new gold leaf glaze
over the other colors, slightly
overlapping them. Use less
new gold leaf than the other
colors. Keep in mind that you
want to see all three colors —
do not blend or muddy them.

6. While the glazes are still
moist, fill the eye dropper
with rubbing alcohol and
splash the alcohol on the
surface, shaking the eye
dropper like a salt shaker.
Immediately, the glazes will
start to spot, separate, puddle, and form craters. The
appearance will vary, de-
pending on how much
alcohol you use. Let dry.

Trim and Finish:

1. Using the photo as a
guide, paint trim areas and
drawer pulls with new gold
leaf glaze. Let dry.

2. Spray with matte sealer.

3. Replace drawer pulls.

1 Prepare and paint surface. Let dry. Pour the acrylic craft paint, latex wall paint, or colored glaze into the glazing medium and mix thoroughly. The amount of paint needed will depend on the depth of color you desire; more paint will give a darker color. Adding the paint to the glazing medium will result in a longer drying time, therefore allowing you more time to do the combing. Pour the glaze mixture onto a disposable plate.

2 Brush a coat of the glaze mixture onto the painted project surface using a foam brush, a bristle brush, or — for larger surfaces — a small paint roller. The thickness of the coat of glaze will create different effects when you comb. Work on one small area at a time since you must manipulate the glaze with the comb before the glaze starts to dry.

3 Comb the surface with long, smooth strokes. If you hesitate, the combed pattern will show where you stopped and started. The side of the comb(s) to be used is specified in individual project instructions. Wipe the edge of the comb with paper towels after each stroke to prevent glaze buildup.

Clean the comb(s) thoroughly with soap and water after each use before the glaze dries. To remove dried glaze from a comb, soak the comb overnight in rubbing alcohol and rinse thoroughly. This will remove the dried glaze only if it has dried within a couple of hours. It will not remove glaze that has been dried for days or weeks.

How to Create Comb Textures

Wiggly waves using a multi-purpose comb

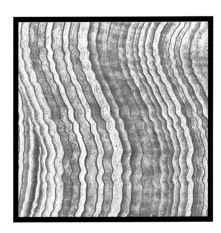

Shimmery waves using a multi-purpose comb

Stripes using a multi-purpose comb or standard comb

Graduated wavy lines using a graduated comb

Curved lines using a graduated comb

Straight line graduated plaid using a graduated comb

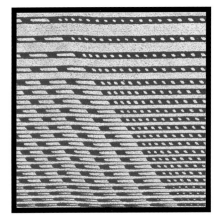

Diagonal cross-hatch plaid using a graduated comb

Scallops using a graduated comb

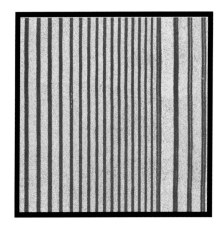

Graduated stripes using a graduated comb

Working in Tight Areas

If you are combing next to moldings or in tight, close areas (like shelves), you may need to trim your comb so the combed texture will reach into corners. Working on a firm surface, trim the comb with a craft knife.

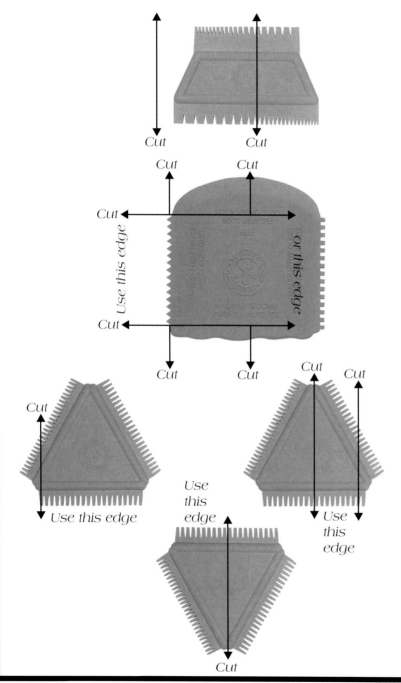

Apothecary Chest

Pictured on page 43.

Designed by
Susan Goans Driggers

This chest uses a variety of combing techniques and all the edges of a multi-purpose comb to create the various designs on the drawer fronts.

GATHER THESE SUPPLIES

Wooden apothecary chest

Paint:
Glazing medium: neutral
Colored glaze: malachite green
Acrylic craft paint: pure gold and robin's egg

Tools:
Sponge brush, 1"
Multi-purpose comb

Other Supplies:
Masking tape
Matte spray sealer

INSTRUCTIONS

Prepare:

1. Remove drawer pulls.

2. Prepare apothecary chest. See "Surface Preparation," pages 7-9.

3. Paint apothecary chest with one or two coats of robin's egg acrylic craft paint. Let dry.

4. Using the photo on page 43 as a guide for color placement, tape off the areas for gold trim.

5. Paint trim areas and drawer pulls with pure gold acrylic craft paint. Let dry. Remove tape.

Glaze and Comb the Apothecary Chest:

1. Mix one part malachite green glaze with one part glazing medium.

2. Using a 1" sponge brush, apply glaze mixture to one area of the drawer fronts at a time, smoothing the glaze out over the surface as you brush. While the glaze is still wet, comb through the glaze. Use different sides of the comb and different combing techniques so each of the drawer fronts is different. Glaze and comb until drawer fronts are completed.

3. Working one area at a time, glaze and comb the sides, front edges, and top of the apothecary chest with long straight lines using the marquetry edge of the comb. Allow the straight lines to cross at the corners on the top.

4. Use the malachite edge of the comb to create the design along the edges of the top, Apply glaze and comb only one side at a time. Let dry.

Finish:

1. Spray with matte sealer.

2. Replace drawer pulls.

Blue Gingham Breakfast Table

Pictured on page 45.

Designed by
Susan Goans Driggers

This breakfast table is a charming place to begin the day. The gingham effect is achieved with two different intensities of the same glaze color.

GATHER THESE SUPPLIES

Round wooden table,
    36" diameter

Paint:
Glazing medium: neutral
Colored glaze: plate blue
Acrylic craft paint:
    parchment and
    wicker white

Tools:
Foam brushes
Multi-purpose comb
Ruler and pencil

Other Supplies:
Masking tape
Matte spray sealer

INSTRUCTIONS

Prepare:

1. Prepare table. See "Surface Preparation," pages 7-9.

2. Paint table top, sides of legs, and larger areas of center pedestal with two or three coats of wicker white acrylic craft paint. Let dry.

3. Paint edges of table top, trim areas of legs, and trim areas of center pedestal with two or three coats of parchment acrylic craft paint. Let dry.

Glaze and Comb the Table:

1. Measure and mark off 5" squares on the table top. One at a time, tape off each square.

2. In one container, mix one part plate blue glaze with one part glazing medium to make glaze mixture for the dark checks, the legs, and the center pedestal.

3. In another container, mix one part plate blue glaze with two parts glazing medium to make glaze mixture for the light checks.

4. Apply the dark colored glaze mixture to alternate squares on table top, one square at a time. Comb in a vertical direction using the marquetry edge of the comb. Let dry. Use the photo on page 45 as a guide.

5. Apply a second coat of the dark colored glaze mixture to the same squares. Comb in a horizontal direction using the marquetry edge of the comb. Let dry. Remove tape.

6. Repeat the procedure using the light colored glaze mixture on remaining squares.

7. Carefully brush the glaze mixture on and comb the leg and center pedestal areas. Use a damp cloth to wipe the glaze off the areas you aren't going to comb. Let dry.

Option:
   Use masking tape to mask off the leg and center pedestal areas that are to be combed. Glaze and comb. Let dry. Remove tape.

Finish:

1. Spray with matte sealer.

Mopping Techniques

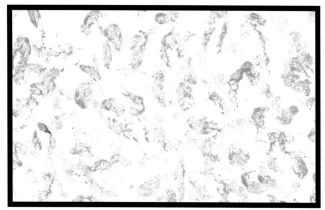

Patina glaze on white paint

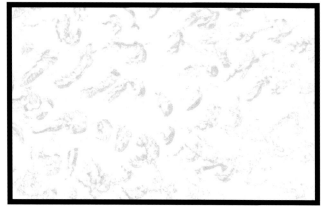

Shrimp bisque glaze on white paint

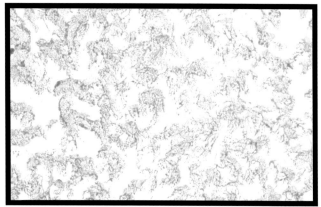

Plate blue glaze on white paint

Mopping uses a tool with strings like those of a household mop to add irregular texture and color to surfaces. As with sponging and ragging, the look of the finished surface depends on the texture of the tool, the colors you choose, and the amount of the background color you let show through. Mopping is especially easy if you use a mopping mitt.

SUPPLIES YOU WILL NEED

Paint:

The type of paint used for mopping should be slightly transparent and have a longer drying time than regular acrylic paint. This can be achieved by mixing an acrylic paint with a glazing medium or paint conditioner. A variety of acrylic paint types can be mixed with the glazing medium: acrylic craft paint, latex wall paint, and colored glaze. Ratios for mixing should follow the manufacturer's directions. Pre-mixed sponging paints can also be used.

Tools:

Mops and mopping mitts can be used.

A trimmed string dish mop is useful for creating a mopped finish on smaller surfaces, such as borders, furniture, and accessories. You can also create a mopped finish using a household string mop. Trim the strings of the mop with scissors and saw off the handle to a convenient length.

Mopping mitts make it very convenient to create a mopped finish without messy hands. These mopping mitts are available at hardware and craft stores.

Using A Mopping Mitt

1 Prepare and paint surface. Let dry. Pour the acrylic craft paint, latex wall paint, or colored glaze into the glazing medium or paint conditioner and mix thoroughly. The amount of paint needed will depend on the depth of color you desire; more paint will give a darker color. Adding the paint to the glazing medium will result in a slightly transparent paint that has a longer drying time, therefore allowing you more time to do the mopping.

2 Always begin with a damp mopping mitt. Dip the mitt into water, then squeeze out as much water as possible. Pour a small amount of glaze mixture onto a disposable plate. Place the mitt on your hand and press the mop string face of the mitt into the glaze mixture to load paint onto the mitt. After loading the mitt, blot the surface of the mitt onto a clean disposable plate to distribute the paint.

3 Pat the mitt onto the surface randomly and repeatedly. Move the mitt over the surface, patting and slightly overlapping each application. Change hand positions frequently. Reload and rinse the mitt to remove glaze buildup as needed.

Mopping mitt:
Mop strings are attached
to a fabric mitt.

Mopped and Combed Wall

Pictured on page 47.

Designed by
Susan Goans Driggers

Mushroom glaze was mixed with glazing medium to create this wall. The upper wall has a mopped finish. The chair rail and the lower wall were combed with a graduated comb.

GATHER THESE SUPPLIES

Paint:
Latex wall paint,
   flat finish: ivory
Glazing medium: neutral
Colored glaze: mushroom

Tools:
Mop or mopping mitt
Graduated comb
Spirit level
Ruler and pencil

Other Supplies:
Masking tape

INSTRUCTIONS

Prepare:

1.   Prepare wall. See "Surface Preparation," pages 7-9.

2.   Paint wall with ivory latex wall paint. Let dry.

3.   Measure and mark lines for chair rail. The chair rail should be the width of the graduated comb plus 1 1/2". Using a spirit level, make certain horizontal lines are straight. Tape off below upper line and above lower line.

Mop the Upper Wall:

1.   Mix mushroom glaze with glazing medium to desired shade.

2.   Mop the upper wall with glaze mixture. Let dry.

Comb the Lower Wall:

1.   Working one section at a time, roll the glaze mixture onto the lower wall. Immediately comb wavy vertical stripes.

2.   Repeat the procedure until lower wall is complete. Let dry. Remove tape.

Comb the Chair Rail:

1.   Tape off above and below the chair rail area.

2.   Apply glaze mixture onto wall between lines of tape.

3.   Using the photo on page 47 as a guide, comb the chair rail. Position the comb so there will be a narrow stripe of glaze at the top and a wider stripe of glaze at the bottom. Let dry. Remove tape.

Mopped Sunroom

Pictured on page 49.

Designed by
Susan Goans Driggers

Rose-colored glaze gives a cheerful hue to this bright sunroom. The mopped texture is highly contrasting and gives a casual feeling that adds to the ambiance of this room.

GATHER THESE SUPPLIES

Paint:
Latex wall paint,
   flat finish: white
Glazing medium: neutral
Colored glaze: roseberry

Tools:
Mop or mopping mitt

INSTRUCTIONS

Prepare:

1.   Prepare walls. See "Surface Preparation," pages 7-9.

2.   Paint walls with white latex wall paint. Let dry.

Mop the Walls:

1.   Mix roseberry glaze with glazing medium to desired shade.

2.   Mop the walls with glaze mixture. Let dry.

Stenciling Techniques

Stenciling is a centuries-old decorative technique of applying paint to a surface through cutout areas of a stiff, paint-resistant material. Stenciling can be used to decorate almost any surface, including walls, furniture, accessories, and floor cloths.

Stenciling using pouncing technique

Stenciling using circular stroke technique

STENCILING ON WALLS

Any wall surface can be stenciled as long as it does not have a waxed or glossy surface.

Plaster and Drywall:

Plaster or drywall surfaces should be painted with two coats of a quality oil or latex wall paint that has a flat finish. Allow paint to cure for at least 24 hours before stenciling.

Flat or satin finish paints are preferable to semi-gloss paint which repels moisture. If you wish to stencil over semi-gloss paint, first lightly spray the surface with a matte sealer. If a glossy wall finish is desired, paint the surface with a latex wall paint with a flat finish; do all your stenciling, then cover the entire surface with a waterbase urethane. This is recommended for bathrooms and kitchens where frequent scrubbing may be necessary.

Textured Walls:

Textured walls can enhance natural color variations in a stenciled print. For example, a pouncing stroke on a sponged wall will have a fresco look.

The degree of texture will affect your choice of stencil design. Generally, open, flowing designs are more attractive on textured walls. If a design features many tiny motifs, the texture of the wall might disturb the continuity of the print. If in doubt, test the design on a small area that can be easily painted over if you decide the design is wrong for your room.

Wood or Plywood Paneling:

Before stenciling a paneled room, try your design on a sample piece of paneling first. Prepare the surface areas, do the stenciling, then apply a finish. If necessary, make adjustments before you begin the actual project.

If you are working on unfinished wood, apply a base stain or clear wood sealer. If you are working on pre-finished paneling, wash it first to remove any wax or dirt. If the paneling has a dark stain, first stencil the design in white or a very light color. Let dry. Then stencil the design in your chosen colors. This technique, called "reversing the color," can be used when you wish to stencil on any dark colored background.

If your paneling has a factory-applied gloss finish, paint may not adhere to it. You can either paint the paneling first with a bonder/primer and then with any latex wall paint with a flat finish or apply a flat varnish before you begin the stenciling process. In either case, once paint or varnish is completely dry and cured, continue with your stenciling, then apply a gloss varnish to the entire surface to restore the sheen.

After stenciling, wait at least three days before applying the finish coats of varnish or polyurethane. Test a small section before applying polyurethane, as oil-base polyurethane has a tendency to yellow with age.

Painted Wood:

If necessary, scrape off loose paint. Sand all wood surfaces and wipe away all dust residue. If furniture is varnished, apply a coat of bonder/primer.

Paint with two or three coats of oil or latex wall paint. Let dry and sand between coats. Proceed with stenciling and let dry.

Apply a waterbase finish according to manufacturer's directions. Oil-base polyurethane can cause the surface to yellow.

Unfinished or Stripped Wood:

Sand all wood surfaces and wipe away all dust residue.

Following manufacturer's directions, apply stain or clear wood sealer. Let dry. Proceed with stenciling and let cure for at least 24 hours.

Apply an oil or waterbase finish according to manufacturer's directions.

STENCILING ON FABRIC

To remove sizing from fabric, wash and dry following manufacturer's directions. Press.

To keep fabric from moving while stenciling, place a piece of extra fine sandpaper underneath the fabric. Position the stencil overlay with tape and/or stencil adhesive. Using a removable fabric pen or tailor's chalk, mark guidelines for the print(s).

When using a brush for stenciling, load brush and stencil as you would on any other surface. Use a variety of strokes and work the paint into the fabric. Repeat with succeeding overlays. Let dry for at least 24 hours.

When using a roller for stenciling, use a textile medium for priming the roller and mix all stencil paint colors with textile medium before applying. Make certain the paint is evenly distributed on the roller so there won't be globs of paint to soak immediately into the fabric. Begin with a very light back and forth stroke, then add more pressure to complete the print. Repeat with succeeding overlays. Let dry for at least 24 hours.

Always work by moving the stenciling fabric away from you, allowing it to drape unfolded over the opposite end of your work surface as it dries.

To finish, heat-set with a dry iron using a pressing cloth. You can heat-set large pieces of fabric by tumble-drying them on the high-heat setting of your clothes dryer. Launder as you would any colored fabric.

How to Stencil

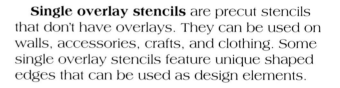

SUPPLIES YOU WILL NEED

Stencils:

Background stencils for background designs have repeated motifs and were designed especially for creating backgrounds. The designs can be used alone or combined with other background stencils or stencil designs.

Single overlay stencils are precut stencils that don't have overlays. They can be used on walls, accessories, crafts, and clothing. Some single overlay stencils feature unique shaped edges that can be used as design elements.

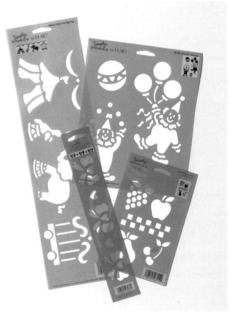

Multi-overlay stencils are precut with one overlay per color. Design registration marks on each sheet make it easy to align the overlays for professional-looking results. Some multi-overlay wall stencils have coordinating spot motif stencils that are perfectly sized for stenciling decorative accessories.

Colorized laser cut stencils are multi-overlay laser cut stencils without bridges or spaces between the cutout shapes. The theorem-type designs use common-line placement, with a progressive buildup of elements to complete each design. Each overlay is printed in color, making it easy to see how the cutout areas can be shaded and blended into the total design. Some designs also include stencils for random elements, making it easy to add spot motifs or design free-flowing repeats.

Paints:

Dry brush stencil paints combine quality and convenience. Their creamy, no-drip formulation makes them easy to use on walls, fabric, and wood surfaces. They are not a good choice for stenciling on a surface with a high sheen.

Paint crayons are stencil paints in stick form. They are easy to apply and quick and neat to use. They are available individually and in sets.

Acrylic craft paints offer quick drying time and a wide variety of premixed colors. With acrylics, it is also easy to mix your own custom colors to coordinate with home decor. On most surfaces, if you make a mistake you can wipe off the paint before it dries and start over.

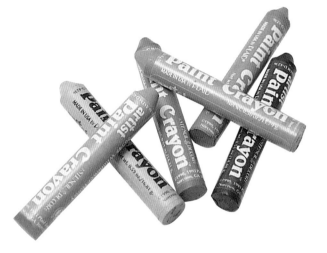

Stencil gel is a gel-like stencil paint which produces a translucent, watercolor look. Its thick formulation holds well on a brush or roller, and it can be blended, toned, and shaded with ease.

Brushes:

Stencil brushes are available in a variety of sizes. The size of the brush you use depends on the size of the openings in your stencil. To stencil a small, delicate print, you might choose a $1/4$" brush; stenciling a large design might require a 1" brush. You need to have a separate brush for each color you plan to stencil in one day. To achieve quality stencil prints, you must let your brush dry thoroughly before you use it again after cleaning.

Bristle brushes have densely packed natural fibers for smooth, soft blending, and solid wood handles. They are perfect for stenciling on fabrics and hard surfaces.

Sponge brushes for stenciling are round sponges on a handle. They can be used to swirl or pounce paint on a variety of surfaces, including fabric. Sponge brushes work well with acrylic craft paints, but they can also be used with dry brush stencil paints and paint crayons. With acrylic craft paints, a sponge brush can be used wet. Therefore, you do not need a separate brush for each paint color.

When you have finished with your sponge brushes, proper cleanup of your brushes is important. When using acrylic craft paint, dry brush stencil paint, or a paint crayon, rinse the brush in warm, soapy water, then squeeze it dry with a towel. You can immediately use the brush again. However, when using oil paint, clean the brush with a solvent that is recommended by the paint manufacturer. Let the sponge brush dry completely before you use it again.

Rollers are ideal for achieving quick background prints and covering background areas. The roller also protects the delicate areas of the stencil and works well in areas of the stencil where using a brush could cause the stencil to move.

Using Acrylic Craft Paints with Stencil Brushes

1 Prepare and paint surface. Let dry. Squeeze some acrylic craft paint onto a disposable plate. Hold the stencil brush at a 90° angle and dip the tips of the brush bristles into the paint to load paint onto the brush. Try to get most of the paint in the center of the brush.

2 Swirl the brush on a paper towel to remove most of the paint. Stenciling is a dry brushing technique, therefore, most mistakes are made by having too much paint on the brush.

3 Swirl the paint onto the uncut portion of the stencil to determine if you have the right amount of paint. Once you have the correct amount, swirl the paint into the cutout areas of the stencil.

Multi-overlay stencil stenciled with appropriate colors of acrylic craft paint

Using Acrylic Craft Paints with Sponge Brushes

1 Prepare and paint surface. Let dry. Squeeze some acrylic craft paint onto a disposable plate. Dip the brush into the paint to load paint onto the brush. Blot the brush on a paper towel to remove most of the paint.

2 Swirl the paint onto the uncut portion of the stencil to determine if you have the right amount of paint. Once you have the correct amount, swirl the paint into the cutout areas of the stencil for a smooth finish or pounce the paint into the cutout areas for a sponged-look finish.

Using Dry Brush Stencil Paints

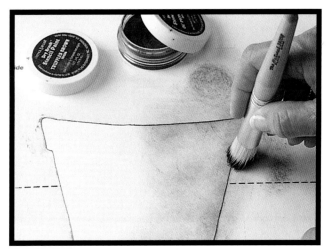

1 Prepare and paint surface. Let dry. A seal automatically forms on the dry brush stencil paint when it has not been used for awhile. To remove this seal, gently scrape the top of the paint with the brush handle. Swirl the brush into the paint to load paint onto the brush.

2 Swirl the paint onto the uncut portion of the stencil to disperse the paint evenly through the brush bristles. Do this each time you load the brush. Swirl the paint into the cutout areas of the stencil. Concentrate the paint on the edges for a shaded effect.

Using Paint Crayons

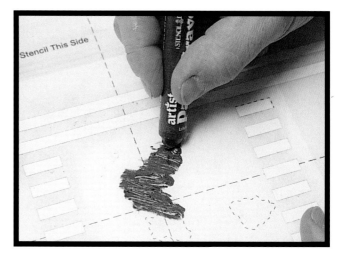

1 Prepare and paint surface. Let dry. A seal automatically forms on the paint crayon when it has not been used for awhile. To remove this seal, gently rub the top of the crayon on a paper towel.

2 Apply the paint crayon to the uncut portion of the stencil. Never apply the paint directly on a cutout area.

3 Using a circular motion, pick up paint from the uncut portion of the stencil with the brush bristles. Work the paint to disperse the paint evenly through the brush bristles. Swirl the paint into the cutout areas of the stencil, using gentle pressure to avoid a buildup of paint along the edges of the cutouts.

Pansy border made using a border stencil and paint crayons

Using Paints with a Stencil Roller

1 Prepare and paint surface. Let dry. At the beginning of a project, prime a dry roller by misting the roller with water, then towel dry. Squeeze about one teaspoon of painting medium onto a disposable plate. The painting medium serves as a base for the color and helps keep the paint from drying out. Roll the roller in the painting medium.

2 Squeeze out two shades of paint from the paint list onto the disposable plate. Roll the primed roller through the two shades of paint. Distribute the paint throughout the roller so it is evenly covered with paint. Keep the two colors from blending completely on the roller by moving the roller back and forth in the same direction. Roll the roller on paper towels to remove excess paint.

3 Beginning with a light stroke, roll roller back and forth over stencil to test the amount of paint, allowing the two colors to create natural shading. You can direct the shading by positioning the roller in different directions over the cutout.

4 The finished stencil.

Using Paints on Wall Border Paper

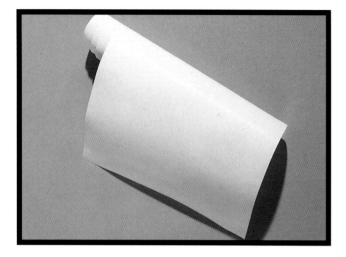

1 Wall border paper makes it easy to stencil a border. You can stencil the design on the paper and then hang the border on the wall. Stenciling can be done with acrylic craft paints, dry brush stencil paints, or paint crayons. If you are using dry brush stencil paints or paint crayons, let the paper roll up loosely as you stencil. When you've finished the first color, stand the roll on its end. Let dry for 24 hours.

2 If you are using acrylic craft paint. Unroll two yards of wall border paper onto a work surface. Tape the stencil you have chosen to the border paper. Moving the stencil along the paper, stencil the first color.

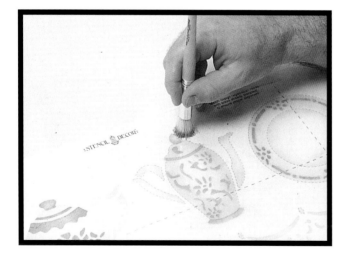

3 Repeat the procedure stenciling with the second color. Let dry to the touch before letting the paper roll up. Let paper cure for 48 hours. Seal the wall border paper with matte sealer before applying to the wall.

4 Starting in an inconspicuous corner of the room, apply wall border paper to wall following manufacturer's directions.

Using Single Overlay Stencils

1 To stencil with one color, position the stencil on the wall and stencil until all the openings are stenciled. Reposition the stencil for repeating the design and extending the border. Repeat the procedure until the entire desired area has been stenciled.

2 To stencil with one color with the addition of shaded edges, position the stencil on the wall and stencil until all the openings are stenciled. Shade edges of the design with the same color family before moving the stencil. Reposition the stencil for repeating the design and extending the border. Repeat the procedure until the entire desired area has been stenciled.

3 To stencil with two colors, position the stencil on the wall and tape off areas in which you do not want the first color of paint to go. Stencil with the first color until all the openings are stenciled. If necessary, move the stencil to stencil any repeats of that color. Remove the tape and tape over the areas that have been stenciled with the first color. Stencil with the second color until all the openings are stenciled.

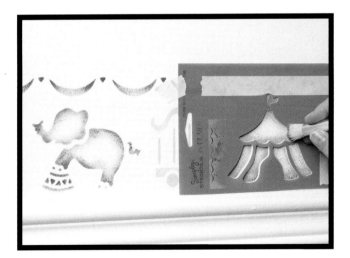

Ivy Wall

Pictured on page 65.

Designed by
Susan Goans Driggers

Vines of ivy leaves frame this arched-top window. The design continues on the walls along the top of the chair rail.

GATHER THESE SUPPLIES

Paint:
Dry brush stencil paint:
    herb garden green and
    vanity teal

Tools:
Stencil brush

Other Supplies:
Multi-overlay stencil:
    ivy border
Stencil tape

INSTRUCTIONS

Stencil the Ivy:

1.   Stencil the simple border design repeatedly along chair rail and around window with herb garden green dry brush stencil paint.

2.   Highlight edges around ivy leaves with vanity teal dry brush stencil paint.

Child's Table Set and Matching Walls

Pictured on page 67.

Designed by
Susan Goans Driggers

What child wouldn't be delighted with this bright and cheery stenciled room and coordinating table and chairs? The scalloped border creates a stenciled chair rail on the sponged wall and the stenciled heart grid gives the look of wallpaper.

GATHER THESE SUPPLIES

Child's table and chairs

Paint:
Latex wall paint,
    flat finish: white
Glazing medium: neutral
Colored glaze: tuscan sunset
Acrylic craft paint: lavender,
    lemon custard, patina,
    pink, and purple lilac
Dry brush stencil paint:
    bouquet pink, English
    lavender, sunny brooke
    yellow, and vanity teal

Tools:
Sea sponge or
    sea sponge mitt
Stencil brushes
Foam brush, 1"
Round artists' brush
Ruler and pencil
Chalk pencil

Other Supplies:
Background stencil:
    hearts and checks
Border stencils: eyelet hearts
    and scalloped heart
Stencil tape
Matte spray sealer

INSTRUCTIONS

Prepare the Table and Chairs:

1.   Prepare table and chairs. See "Surface Preparation," pages 7-9.

2.   Paint table and chairs with two or three coats of white latex wall paint. Let dry and sand between coats.

3.   Using the 1" foam brush and the round artists' brush and the photo on page 67 as a guide for color placement, paint the trim on the table and chairs with lavender, lemon custard, patina, pink, and purple lilac acrylic craft paint.

Stencil the Table and Chairs:

1.   Using a chalk pencil, position the scalloped edge of the eyelet hearts border stencil 3" to 4" from the edge of the table.

2.   Load sea sponge or sea sponge mitt with lemon custard acrylic craft paint. Blot sponge on a scrap piece of paper to remove excess paint — you want a faint shading of color for stenciling.

3.   Sponge the edge of the stencil allowing the color to fade toward the edge of the table top. Measure and stencil the sides then connect the design at the corners. Let dry.

4.   Using the eyelet hearts border stencil and a stencil brush, stencil the design within the border with bouquet pink, English lavender, sunny brooke yellow, and vanity teal dry brush stencil paint. Use the photo as a guide for color and design placement.

5.   Using the same colors and the motifs from the eyelet hearts border stencil, stencil the seats of the chairs.

6.   Using the small heart section on the hearts and checks background stencil, stencil the chair backs and the tops of the chairs' legs with English lavender dry brush stencil paint.

7.   Stencil a row of small hearts across the top of each chair back with bouquet pink dry brush stencil paint.

8. Using the small and large heart sections on the hearts and checks background stencil, stencil hearts on the chair seats and around the edge of the table top.

9. Let paint cure for three to five days.

Finish:

1. Spray table and chairs with matte sealer.

Prepare the Walls:

1. Prepare walls. See "Surface Preparation," pages 7-9.

2. Paint walls with white latex wall paint. Let dry.

Sponge the Walls:

1. Mix tuscan sunset glaze with glazing medium to desired shade.

2. Sponge walls with glaze mixture. Let dry.

Stencil the Walls:

1. Measure and mark walls 34" up from the floor and mark placement for the stenciled border.

2. At the marked line, position the scalloped heart border stencil on the wall.

3. Stencil border design with bouquet pink, English lavender, and sunny brooke yellow dry brush stencil paint. Use the photo as a guide for color placement.

4. Before stenciling the hearts on the wall below the border, mark off a 2" grid of horizontal and vertical lines. The hearts were not used as they are positioned on the border stencil — instead, they were stenciled on the grid where the lines intersect.

5. Stencil the hearts with English lavender dry brush stencil paint using both large and small hearts. For the first horizontal row, stencil a large heart at every other intersecting vertical line of grid. All stenciled hearts should be centered.

6. For the row of small hearts, use the next horizontal line. Stencil a small heart at every other intersecting vertical line, placing each below and between the large hearts on the row above.

7. Repeat the procedure, alternating rows of large and small hearts, until the entire bottom area of the walls is stenciled.

Ivy Lattice Table

Pictured on page 68.

Designed by
Susan Goans Driggers

This table is painted with two colors, then stenciled with two designs. The light blue-green color sets the stage for a golden stenciled lattice background. Darker green ivy leaves are stenciled over the lattice on the table top and legs.

GATHER THESE SUPPLIES

Oval wooden side table

Paint:
Acrylic craft paint: hunter green and robin's egg
Dry brush stencil paint: gold metallic and sherwood forest green

Tools:
Stencil brush

Other Supplies:
Background stencil: lattice collection
Border stencil: ivy swag
Stencil tape
Matte spray sealer

INSTRUCTIONS

Prepare:

1. Prepare table. See "Surface Preparation," pages 7-9.

2. Paint table top, apron, and outer portions of legs with two or three coats of robin's egg acrylic craft paint. Let dry and sand between coats.

3. Paint the lower shelf and inner portions of legs with two coats of hunter green acrylic craft paint. Let dry and sand between coats.

Stencil the Table:

1. Using the cross-hatch lattice section on the lattice collection background stencil, stencil the lattice with gold metallic dry brush stencil paint on the parts of the table that have been painted with robin's egg acrylic craft paint.

2. Using the stencil brush, apply gold metallic dry brush stencil paint along the rim of the table top.

3. Using the ivy swag border stencil, stencil the ivy on the table top and at tops of legs with sherwood forest green dry brush stencil paint. Use the photo as a guide for design placement.

4. Let paint cure for three to five days.

Finish:

1. Spray table with matte sealer.

Using Multi-Overlay Stencils

1 Stencils with more than one overlay have registration marks printed on them so they can be lined up properly. One overlay is used for one color; the next overlay is used for another color. The overlays are marked A, B, C, etc. and they should be used in order.

Use the overlay marked "A" to stencil the first color.

2 Line up the registration marks and stencil the second color with the overlay marked "B".

3 Line up the registration marks and stencil the third color with the overlay marked "C".

4 The finished stencil.

Embellishing Stencils with Paint Brushes

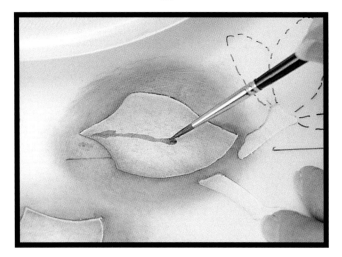

1 Stencil the leaves with a solid color of acrylic craft paint or with a mixture of two or more colors of acrylic craft paint. Thin the paint or paint mixture with a glazing medium or with water. Using a round artists' brush, paint the veins inside the leaves to embellish.

2 Carefully remove the stencil to see the results.

Magnolia Screen

Pictured on page 71.

Designed by
Jane Gauss

This painted and stenciled room screen is a good example of how stenciled projects can be embellished with decorative painting techniques for detail, depth, and texture. A round artists' brush was used to paint veins on the leaves and to add tendrils. You can create and cut a trellis stencil to fit your screen or purchase a precut stencil.

GATHER THESE SUPPLIES

Three-section room screen

Paint:
Latex wall paint,
    flat finish: off white and
    rosy beige
Glazing medium: neutral
Colored glaze: ivy green and
    sky blue
Acrylic craft paint:
    burnt sienna, burnt umber,
    pure gold metallic, raw
    sienna, ripe avocado,
    southern pine, titanium
    white, and vanilla cream

Tools:
Natural sponge
Stencil brushes
Round artists' brush

Other Supplies:
Multi-overlay stencil:
    magnolia blossoms
Single overlay stencil:
    lattice or
    stencil blank material
Stencil tape
Matte spray sealer

INSTRUCTIONS

Prepare:

1. Remove hinges. Prepare screen. See "Surface Preparation," pages 7-9.

2. Paint screen with off white latex wall paint. Let dry.

Sponge the Screen:

1. Using a natural sponge, sponge the screen with rosy beige latex wall paint. Let dry.

2. Thin the ivy green glaze with water and sponge the lower part of the screen. Use the photo below as a guide for color placement.

3. Mix sky blue glaze with titanium white acrylic craft paint to lighten. Thin with water and sponge the upper part of the screen. Use the photo as a guide for color placement.

Stencil the Screen and Add the Painting Details:

1. Use a lattice multi-overlay stencil or cut a trellis pattern to fit your screen. Using stencil blank material, make your own trellis stencil.

2. Stencil trellis around the sides and top of screen panels with titanium white acrylic craft paint. Let dry.

3. Mix one part ripe avocado acrylic craft paint with one part southern pine acrylic craft paint. Stencil the leaves.

4. Dilute paint mixture with water and paint the veins in the leaves using a round artists' brush.

5. Stencil branches with burnt sienna acrylic craft paint and shade with burnt umber acrylic craft paint.

6. Mix five parts vanilla cream acrylic craft paint with one part burnt sienna acrylic craft paint. Stencil lower flower petals.

7. Stencil middle flower petals with vanilla cream acrylic craft paint.

8. Mix two parts vanilla cream acrylic craft paint with one part titanium white acrylic craft paint. Stencil upper flower petals.

9. Stipple the upper flower petals with pure gold metallic acrylic craft paint.

10. Stencil the flower centers with ripe avocado and southern pine paint mixture plus raw sienna acrylic craft paint.

11. Dilute southern pine acrylic craft paint with water and paint tendrils using a round artists' brush. Hold the brush at the tip of the handle and twist and roll it for a natural flow. Let dry.

Finish:

1. Spray screen with matte sealer and assemble.

Grape Vine Kitchen

Pictured on page 73.

Designed by
Kathi Malarchuk

These grape vines give this kitchen a European country look. The versatile grape border, stenciled with a colorized laser cut stencil, can be used in a variety of ways. The entire border was used on the wall above the cabinets. Random elements from the stencil and parts of the border were used to create the stenciling around the window.

GATHER THESE SUPPLIES

Paint:
Latex wall paint,
  flat finish: white
Stencil gel: fern, napa grape,
  twig, and village green

Tools:
Stencil brushes
Stencil roller

Other Supplies:
Colorized laser cut stencil:
  grape vine
Stencil tape

INSTRUCTIONS

Prepare:

1. Prepare walls. See "Surface Preparation," pages 7-9.

2. Paint walls with white latex wall paint. Let dry.

Stencil the Walls:

1. Stencil the grapes with napa grape stencil gel. Let dry.

2. Stencil the leaves with fern stencil gel and village green stencil gel. Let dry.

3. Stencil the vines with twig stencil gel. Let dry.

Using Disposable Stencil Tape

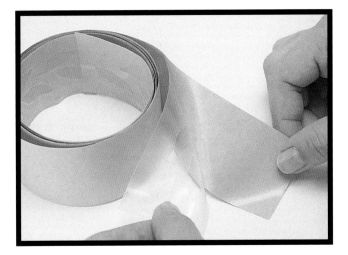

1 Stenciling with disposable stencil tape is quick, easy, and fun. Disposable stencil tape is a clear, sticky-backed, flexible tape with cutout designs. It is great for creating borders, working over curves, and working in narrow spaces on wood, papier mâché, and walls.

Measure the area to be stenciled and cut a piece of disposable stencil tape to the appropriate length. Peel off the paper backing.

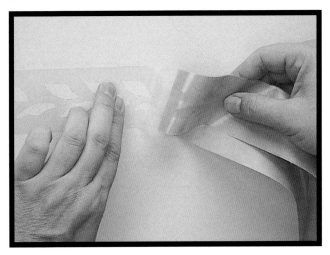

2 Position the disposable stencil tape on the surface. The tape can be repositioned, so if it is not where you want it to be, peel it up and move it. The adhesive back holds it firmly in place.

3 Load a stencil brush with paint. Blot stencil brush on a paper towel to remove excess paint.

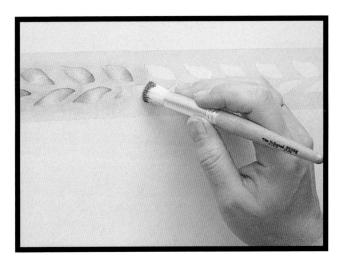

4 Apply paint through the openings. Remove stencil tape before the stencil paint dries completely.

Neoclassic Wall

Pictured on page 77.

Designed by
Susan Goans Driggers

This wall combines two glazed finishes and uses disposable stencil tape designs to create a border on the upper part of the wall.

GATHER THESE SUPPLIES

Paint:
Latex wall paint,
    flat finish: off white
Glazing medium: neutral
Colored glaze: mushroom and
    russet brown
Stencil gel: king's gold and
    russet

Tools:
Rags or ragging mitt
Stencil brushes
Ruler and pencil
Spirit level

Other Supplies:
Disposable stencil tape:
    beads and bars run;
    egg and dart
Masking tape

INSTRUCTIONS

Prepare:

1. Prepare wall. See "Surface Preparation," pages 7-9.

2. Paint wall with off white latex wall paint. Let dry.

Rag the Wall:

1. Measure and mark wall 18" down from the ceiling or crown molding and mark placement for the stenciled border. Using a spirit level, tape off a line below the marks.

2. Mix two parts russet brown glaze with three parts glazing medium.

3. Using rags or a ragging mitt, rag upper part of wall with glaze mixture. Work in an area about three feet wide. Let it set up a little, then go back and rub and pat again for a more rubbed, burnished look. Repeat the procedure until the entire upper part of the wall is glazed. Remove tape. Let dry for 24 hours.

4. Tape off wall above marked line.

5. Mix one part mushroom glaze with five parts glazing medium.

6. Using rags or a ragging mitt, lightly and sparsely rag lower part of wall with glaze mixture. Immediately pat again to disperse color for a rag-rolled look. Repeat the procedure until the entire lower part of the wall is glazed. Remove tape. Let dry for 24 hours.

Stencil the Wall:

1. Position the beads and bars run disposable stencil tape below the marked line at the top edge of the light part of the wall. Stencil with king's gold stencil gel. Let dry.

2. Shade edges of beads and bars with russet stencil gel. Remove tape. Let dry.

3. Position the egg and dart disposable stencil tape under the beads and bars run stenciled border. Stencil with the same colors. Remove tape. Let dry.

Creating Cobblestone

1 **Sponge on mortar.** Use a sea sponge to sponge the background with the mortar color. Here, black and white stencil gel was used to create the gray mortar. The sponging creates a mottled, textured look.

2 **Stencil stones.** Position the cobblestone stencil. Load the stencil roller and apply the base color. For cobblestone, mix shadow gray stencil gel with either taupe or black stencil gel. Reposition the stencil until you have finished the entire area with the base color.

3 **Sponge on additional colors.** Reposition the stencil and use a sea sponge to sponge additional colors or to create a textured look on the stone or brick. Sponge wet on wet colors, randomly adding colors so each stone is different: These stencil gel colors were used here: berry red, white, black, russet, and taupe.

4 **Add shadows.** Add shadows on edges with a mixture of black stencil gel and glazing medium. Stencil in a tight, circular stroke around the edges.

Cobblestone Floorcloth on Vinyl

Pictured on page 79.

Designed by
Jane Gauss

Embellished with ivy, this cobblestone floorcloth is a practical and inexpensive way to create a unique rug that will withstand heavy traffic and wipe clean with a damp cloth. It is stenciled on the back of a vinyl flooring scrap rather than on canvas.

GATHER THESE SUPPLIES

Scrap of vinyl flooring —
   you are going to stencil the back of this vinyl so the pattern doesn't matter. Select a good quality flooring that does not have a paper backing.

Paint:

Latex wall paint,
   satin finish: off white
Glazing medium: neutral
Stencil gel: berry red, black, russet, shadow gray, taupe, village green, white, and wild ivy
Waterbase sealer/primer
Waterbase urethane varnish, satin finish

Tools:

Sea sponge
Paint roller
Heavy-duty scissors

Other Supplies:

Multi-overlay stencil: cobblestone and ivy
Stencil tape
Tack cloth
Damp cloth
Brown paper bags

INSTRUCTIONS

Prepare the Vinyl:

1. Using heavy-duty scissors, cut vinyl slightly larger than you want the floorcloth to be.

2. Using a paint roller, apply two coats of waterbase sealer/primer to the back of the vinyl. Let dry.

3. Paint the primed surface with two coats of off white latex wall paint. Let dry.

Sponge on Mortar:

1. Using a damp sponge, sponge entire surface of floorcloth with black and white stencil gel to create mortar. This will give the area an uneven, mottled look. Let dry.

Stencil the Stones:

1. To make the base color, mix equal amounts of russet stencil gel and glazing medium. Position the stencil in approximate center of the rug and roll on the base color. Turn the stencil as you work from the center and randomly place the stones. You do not want the look of a repeated pattern. Let dry.

To cover a large area, have a quart of latex wall paint in the russet color mixed at your local paint store. Mix the latex wall paint with an equal amount of glazing medium and roll the glaze mixture on the surface.

2. Reposition the stencil on cobblestones and sponge wet-on-wet tones of berry red, black, shadow gray, taupe, and white stencil gel. Use the photo as a guide for color placement. Let dry.

You can use other colors from your room and incorporate them into the stone mix.

3. Shadow the edges of the rocks and the mortar with a mixture of black stencil gel and glazing medium. Let dry.

Stencil the Ivy:

1. Using the ivy multi-overlay stencil, stencil the ivy with village green stencil gel and wild ivy stencil gel. Use the photo as a guide for color and design placement. Let dry.

Trim and Finish:

1. Using heavy-duty scissors, cut along the edges of the stenciled stones as shown in the photo to make an uneven edge.

2. Remove any markings or smudges with a damp cloth. Wipe surface with a tack cloth to remove any dust or lint.

3. Roll on one coat of waterbase urethane varnish being careful not to overwork the surface with the roller. *Do not use oil-based polyurethane.* It will discolor and crack on the vinyl surface. Let dry thoroughly.

4. Apply a second coat of urethane varnish, working the roller in several directions, finishing with rolling in one direction. Let dry thoroughly.

5. Lightly "sand" the surface with a crumpled piece of brown paper bag. Wipe with a tack cloth.

6. Apply a third coat of urethane varnish. "Sand" again and wipe with a tack cloth.

7. Apply a fourth coat of urethane varnish. Let cure for 48 hours.

Birdhouse Floorcloth on Canvas

Pictured on page 81.

Designed by
Kathi Malarchuk

This design combines the technique of stenciling with block printing.

See chapter on Block Printing for more details on this technique.

GATHER THESE SUPPLIES

Canvas, 42" x 62" —
   add additional 4" of
   canvas for turning under.

Paint:

Latex wall paint,
   flat finish: white
Glazing medium: neutral
Colored glaze: alpine green,
   plate blue, pumpkin,
   and tuscan sunset
Acrylic craft paint:
   spring white
Dry brush stencil paint:
   black, ecru lace, and
   true blue
Waterbase urethane varnish,
   satin finish
Oil-base polyurethane

Tools:

Ragging mitt
Sponge brushes
Flat brush
#3 round brush
Ruler
Chalk pencil
Artists' eraser
Fabric glue
Rolling pin

Other Supplies:

Block printing design:
   little garden flowers
Multi-overlay stencil:
   birdhouse
Single-overlay stencil:
   backgrounds checkerboard
   collection
Stencil tape
Tack cloth
Masking tape
#0000 steel wool
Liquid latex rug backing

INSTRUCTIONS

Prepare:

1. Using scissors, cut away selvages from canvas.

2. Using a dry iron, iron canvas to remove all wrinkles. *Steam and moisture can cause shrinkage.*

3. Paint the canvas with two coats of white latex wall paint. Let dry thoroughly between coats and let final coat dry for 24 hours.

4. Paint over base coat with one coat of spring white acrylic craft paint. Let dry.

5. On the right side, mark a 1" hem on all four sides with a chalk pencil. Trim any loose threads.

Rag the Canvas:

1. Mix tuscan sunset glaze with glazing medium to a medium shade.

2. Using a ragging mitt, lightly rag over entire surface of canvas with glaze mixture, creating a ragged texture. Let dry for 24 hours.

3. Tape off a 5" border on all sides. Measure 1" from inner edge of border and tape off. Measure 2" from outer edge of floorcloth and tape off. This creates a narrow inner border and a wide outer border.

4. Mix plate blue glaze with glazing medium to a deep shade.

5. Using a ragging mitt, apply glaze mixture on borders inside the taped lines. Remove tape. Let dry.

6. Tape off three rows of five 10" squares.

7. Mix remaining glazing medium with alpine green glaze.

8. Using a ragging mitt, apply glaze mixture on alternate squares. Use the photo on page 81 as a placement guide. Remove tape. Let dry.

Stencil the Birdhouses:

1. Stencil the birdhouse walls with ecru lace dry brush stencil paint.

2. Stencil the birdhouse roofs and bases with true blue dry brush stencil paint.

3. Using the checkerboard stencil, stencil checks on birdhouse walls with true blue dry brush stencil paint.

4. Stencil entrance holes and perches on birdhouses with black dry brush stencil paint.

Block Print the Flowers:

1. Block print small flowers in center square, around birdhouses, and on light band between two blue ragged borders using the small flower petal with plate blue glaze. Use the photo as a placement guide. Let dry.

2. Block print leaves with alpine green glaze. Let dry.

3. Add flower centers with pumpkin glaze. Let dry.

4. Using a #3 round brush, paint stems and tendrils with alpine green glaze mixture. Let dry for 72 hours.

Hem the Canvas:

1. Turn hem under and crease at the line marked with the chalk pencil.

2. Miter the corners. To miter, crease each side out to the edge. Fold up the corner and press.

3. Cut off triangular piece.

4. Remove marked hem lines with an artists' eraser.

5. Apply an even coat of fabric glue to the wrong side of the hem.

6. With a rolling pin, roll one side of the hem at a time to secure and remove air pockets.

7. To prevent the hem from buckling, weight down evenly. Let dry overnight.

Finish:

1. Apply three to five coats of non-yellowing oil-base polyurethane. Drying time between coats should follow the manufacturer's directions. In humid conditions, allow an additional six to eight hours of drying time.

2. After the final coat has dried, rub the surface with #0000 steel wool. Remove dust with a tack cloth.

For Safe Use:

Because floorcloths can be dangerous on slippery floors, use one of these backings for safety:

1. Apply a liquid latex rug backing to the underside of the floorcloth.

2. Secure the entire perimeter of the floorcloth by applying double-faced carpet tape on the underside.

3. Place on a thin-carpet pad that has been designed to help rugs stay put. Don't use a thick pad — a floorcloth can crack if placed on a thick pad or a carpeted floor.

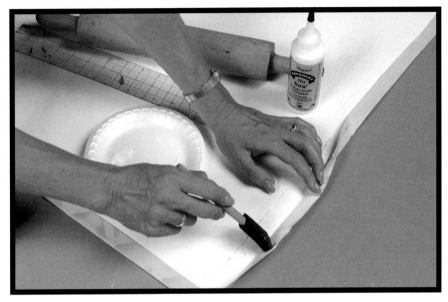

Hemming a floorcloth. Apply glue to the hem area.

Hemming a floorcloth. Roll one side of hem to secure and remove air pockets.

Cutting Your Own Stencil

1 Place stencil blank material over your desired pattern. Trace the pattern onto the stencil blank material with a permanent ink pen.

2 Place the stencil blank material on a glass cutting surface. With a sharp craft knife, cut out the open areas of the design. Move the stencil blank material as you cut rather than moving the knife.

3 **Optional method for cutting:** Place the stencil blank material on the glass cutting surface. Using an electric stencil cutting tool, cut out the open areas of the design.

Stenciled Room Screen

Pictured on page 87.

Designed by
Jane Gauss

This dramatic room screen has faux tortoise shell insets and a gold stenciled design. The design is from the Lakeside Collection compiled by stenciler Jane Gauss. The stencils were found at a cottage in Lakeside, Ohio. Lakeside, a community located on the shore of Lake Erie, was founded as a Methodist campground in the 19th Century. It is believed that this design dates from the period 1895-1910.

GATHER THESE SUPPLIES

Wooden folding room screen

Paint:
Latex wall paint,
    flat finish: black
Glazing medium, neutral
Colored glaze: black,
    new leaf gold, and
    penny copper
Acrylic craft paint:
    antique gold
Stencil gel: king's gold

Tools:
Foam brush
Stencil brush
Sponge brush, 1"
Bristle brush
Eye dropper
Craft knife

Other Supplies:
Stencil blank material
Tracing paper
Permanent ink pen
Sandpaper, 220 grit
Masking tape
Spray bottle
Rubbing alcohol
Stencil tape
Matte spray sealer

INSTRUCTIONS

Prepare:

1. Remove hinges. Prepare screen. See "Surface Preparation," pages 7-9.

2. Paint screen with black latex wall paint. Let dry.

Stencil the Screen:

1. Trace the stencil design onto tracing paper using a permanent ink pen. If necessary, reduce or enlarge pattern to fit your screen.

2. Transfer and cut the stencil design from the stencil blank material.

3. Stencil the design on the screen with king's gold stencil gel. Use the photo on page 87 as a guide. Let dry.

Create the Tortoise Shell Insets:

1. To create the tortoise shell, use a wet-on-wet process. Keep a spray bottle filled with water handy to mist the project periodically as it starts to dry. You want the colored glazes moist, but not runny. It is best to work with the project on a horizontal surface. If your project surface is vertical, keep the glazes a little drier as this will lessen the water-splashed appearance.

2. Tape off areas of your screen where you would like to create the tortoise shell finish. Use the photo as a guide for placement.

3. Using a sponge brush, paint the areas that will receive the tortoise shell finish with antique gold acrylic craft paint. Let dry for two hours.

4. Lightly sand and remove dust. Apply another coat of antique gold acrylic craft paint. Let dry.

5. Brush a coat of glazing medium over the antique gold acrylic craft paint, but do not let it dry!

6. While the surface is moist, use a foam brush to randomly pounce new gold leaf glaze over the glazing medium. Don't completely cover the antique gold base coat. Rinse the foam brush.

7. Apply penny copper glaze over the moist new gold leaf glaze using the same procedure. Rinse the foam brush.

8. Apply black glaze over the other colors using the same procedure. All four colors should show. Don't blend or muddy the colors.

9. Fill the eye dropper with rubbing alcohol. Splash the glazed areas, shaking the eye dropper like a salt shaker. The glazes will immediately start to water spot, separate, puddle, and form craters. The appearance will vary depending on how much alcohol you splash.

10. While the alcohol and glaze colors are still wet, use a bristle brush to work the glaze colors. Wait for five to ten minutes and splash with more alcohol until the result is pleasing. Remove tape. Let dry completely.

Finish:

1. Spray screen with matte sealer and assemble.

Block Printing Techniques

Block printing is an age-old craft that has found new life in home decorating. Traditionally blocks were cut from wood, then later from linoleum. The cut block design is coated with paint or ink then "printed" or pressed onto a surface. Today, this process is made easy for the do-it-yourself home decorator with many innovative, easy-to-use products for block printing.

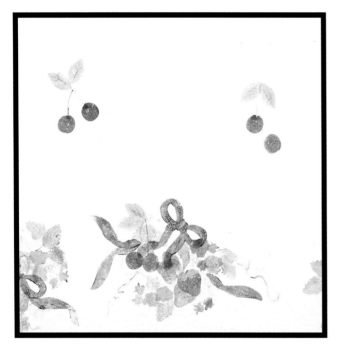

Close-up of block printed fruit bouquets on a white wall

SUPPLIES YOU WILL NEED

Paint:

Colored glazes are the ideal block printing medium. They have a subtle transparency and a gel-like consistency and are waterbase and colorfast on fabrics.

Acrylic craft paints, mixed with a glazing medium, painting medium, or paint conditioner, can also be used for block printing.

SETTING UP YOUR WORK SURFACE AND PREPARING YOUR PALETTE

Set up your work area on a sturdy table covered with paper or plastic. If you are working with many printing blocks, have a container of water with a drop of mild dish detergent in it nearby for cleaning the blocks as you work.

Have your brushes handy. One flat artists' brush can be used to load several colors of paint in the same family. When changing to another color family, swish the brush in water then blot it on an old terry hand towel.

When working on fabrics, cover your table with blank newsprint paper to serve as a blotter. Keep your paints and supplies on another table since smudges are next to impossible to remove from fabrics.

Printing Blocks:

Printing blocks are available at many craft stores, as well as many home improvement stores. The designs are precut in a wide range of designs.

Printing blocks are die-cut from a soft and durable stamping material that is easy to clean and can be used time and time again. Each block has its own handle that makes loading the block with paint and setting the block onto the surface easier. Because they are flexible, you can use printing blocks on just about any surface — around corners, over molding trims, and on most rounded surfaces.

There are designs available for every decorating style, as well as blank block material so you can cut your own designs.

Brushes:

Flat artists' brushes are used for loading the printing blocks with paint. Though one brush can be used for several colors within the same family, you should have two or three loading brushes available.

Round artists' brushes that are pointed are used for painting vines and other details. These brushes must be used when painting vines, tendrils, and stems to any block printed design.

Other Supplies:

Small Bowl of Water: For cleaning brushes and maintaining moisture in printing blocks.

Old Terry Hand Towel: For drying brushes and hand cleanup.

Slightly Moisted Hand Towel: For correcting mistakes. Pre-moistened, pull-up wipes in a dispenser can also be used for this purpose.

Disposable Plate: For use as a palette.

Brown Paper Bag or Smooth Disposable Surface: For blotting paint-loaded printing blocks.

Practice Paper: For practicing the design presses.

Chalk or 1/4" Quilters' Tape: For marking wall surfaces.

Soft Toothbrush or Cellulose Sponge: For cleaning printing blocks.

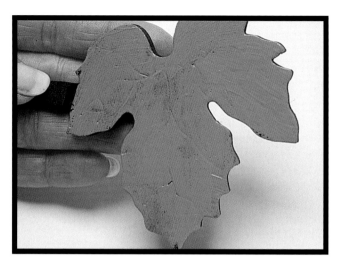

1 Prepare and paint surface. Let dry. Squeeze a dime-sized amount of colored glaze onto a disposable plate. Dip the flat artists' brush in water and blot it on a paper towel to remove excess water. Load the flat brush with paint. Hold the printing block by the handle and apply a thin coat of paint to the cut side. Brush the paint out to the edge of the design, making certain you do not get paint on the handle.

2 More than one color can be added to each block. For example, on an ivy leaf, a dark green can be applied to the edge of the leaf, a medium green to the middle area, and then a light green added in spots for highlighting. If a particular design has a flower or a leaf all on one printing block, simply apply green to the leaf area and a flower color to the flower area.

3 Holding the loaded printing block by the handle, place it on the project surface. Use your other hand to gently press the block against the surface without sliding it. Release the handle as soon as the block touches the surface to avoid sliding the printing block.

4 Use your fingertips to press the block. Let one hand gently hold the block while the fingers of your other hand "walk" around the block.

5 Using the handle, lift the printing block. Move to another section and repeat the procedure. You should be able to produce two to three printed impressions before having to apply more paint to the surface of the printing block. For finishing touches, add vines or other accents with a round artists' brush.

6 To make vines delicate and more transparent than the design, dilute a small amount of vine colored glaze with water or glazing medium. Drag the brush through the diluted paint. Create vines with a light pulling, twisting motion, keeping a loose wrist and fingers. Vines that are too heavy will detract from the overall effect. If the vines are too distinct, remove them with a damp cloth or cotton swab and try again.

Block Printing Walls In Your Home

Preparing the Surface:

Block printing can be done on any painted or stained surface as long as the surface is not deeply textured. The more sheen there is to the surface, the lighter the colors will appear. The best surface to print on is one that is painted with a flat- or satin-finish paint.

If you are working on a wall surface that has not been freshly painted or is wallpapered, wash the wall with a mild cleaner to remove any dirt or grease.

Practice Paper:

Plain newsprint paper or brown paper bags make good practice areas. Print out your design on plain paper, cut out the designs, and tape them to the wall to decide if you like the flow and color of the design before actually printing on your wall.

Layout of the Design:

To lay out the design on your wall, mark the positions of the designs with chalk. However, right before you make each block print, you must wipe the chalk off the wall. If your design is a vining-type design, you can use 1/4" quilters' tape to indicate the vine leaves. This will help you place the leaves along the vine. Remove the tape as you need to work in each area.

When planning your design, remember that leaves should have a natural flow toward the light. Begin at the top of the wall and work down, adjusting your placement every two to three feet. Frequently step back from the project to see how the design is progressing.

When creating borders, avoid rigid, exacting repeats. Allow some vines or motifs to go up onto the ceiling or to drop across molding trim.

1 Prepare and paint surface. Let dry. To lay out the design on your wall, mark the general direction of the vines with chalk or ¼" quilters' tape.

2 Block print the design, wiping off the chalk or removing the tape as you go. Place some leaves over the line of the vine. Add flowers after leaves have been printed. Some leaves can be printed later as fill in or foreground.

3 To finish, remove any remaining chalk or tape. Using a round artists' brush, add vines and tendrils with diluted glaze. Add an occasional random leaf to avoid the look of a repeated pattern.

TIPS FOR BLOCK PRINTING ON FABRIC:

• Choose 100% cotton, cotton-polyester blends, denim, silk, organdy, jersey, linen, burlap, or canvas. Coarse, nubby, or heavily textured fabrics will produce a less defined print. If in doubt, experiment on a scrap or in an inconspicuous place.

• If you are block printing a washable fabric, always wash the fabric before you block print on it. This will remove the sizing.

• Always allow the colored glaze to cure for at least 24 hours before heat setting it. Heat your iron on a dry setting to the heat recommended for the fabric you are using. Cover the block printed area with a pressing cloth and hold the iron on the printed area for 30 seconds. On a very large project, tumble the block printed fabric in the dryer for 30 minutes before you heat set it to be sure all areas receive sufficient heat.

• To launder, turn the project inside out and hand wash or machine wash on a gentle cycle in cool water using a mild laundry detergent. Line dry or dry on a low heat.

Painting Floors In Your Home

Working on Floors:

When working on a floor, protect both your knees and the surface with foam knee pads or a folded terry towel.

The towel is also handy for wiping your hands and for keeping perspiration off the painted surface.

Striping:

When striping, do not leave tape in place for a long period of time. For example, do not apply tape at night, then paint the next day. The tape might pull up the base paint.

Once paint has been applied in a taped-off area, remove the tape within two or three minutes. If the paint is permitted to dry on the tape it can pull off the edge of the stripe when the tape is removed.

When painting a floor of a larger size, paint one side then remove the tape before proceeding to the next side.

If an edge gets smudged or if paint bleeds under the tape, clean up with a slightly moistened cotton swab or a foam eye shadow applicator. The foam applicator is easily rinsed clean; cotton swabs need to be replaced frequently.

Painting Cross-Hatched Stripes

1 Cross-hatched stripes can be used to create a simple checked design or, when positioned diagonally, to create a lattice. For easy striping, make the stripes the width of the masking tape you have chosen. To begin, mark the outer edge and apply a continuous strip of masking tape to the outer edge of the marked line. Apply another piece of masking tape exactly next to the first strip of tape. Apply another piece of masking tape exactly next to the second strip of tape.

2 Now remove the middle strip of tape to create the stripe to be painted. Repeat the procedure until you have taped off all the stripes in one direction. Paint the stripes, remove all the tape, and let dry.

Repeat the procedure for the stripes going in the opposite direction.

Fruit and Bows Kitchen

Pictured on page 95.

Designed by
Jane Gauss and Liza Glenn

Block printed cherries, bows, and fruit bouquets brighten these white kitchen walls.

An assortment of accessories carries out the fruit theme. The area below the chair rail was papered with blue plaid wallpaper.

Fruit and Bows Walls

Pictured on page 95.

GATHER THESE SUPPLIES

Paint:
Latex wall paint,
    flat finish: porcelain white
Colored glaze: bark brown,
    black cherry, burgundy,
    danish blue, deep woods
    green, geranium red,
    lemon yellow, new leaf
    green, and plum

Tools:
Flat artists' brushes
Round artists' brush

Other Supplies:
Block printing designs:
    bows, fruits, and
    mixed berries
Blue plaid wallpaper

INSTRUCTIONS

Prepare:

1. Prepare walls. See "Surface Preparation," pages 7-9.

2. Paint upper walls with porcelain white latex wall paint. Let dry.

3. Paper lower walls with blue plaid wallpaper.

Block Print the Design:

1. Block print the fruit bouquets using the following glaze colors: strawberries — geranium red shaded with burgundy; cherries — black cherry; small flowers — danish blue and plum; petal flowers — lemon yellow; raspberries — plum; leaves — deep woods green and new leaf green. Use the photo on page 95 as a guide for color and design placement.

2. Block print the ribbons on the fruit bouquets with danish blue glaze.

3. Block print the cherries in a random pattern over the entire upper walls. As you block print the cherries, think of the cherries being tossed on the surface. Add an occasional single cherry to fill smaller areas.

4. Using a round artists' brush, paint the stems on the cherries with diluted bark brown glaze.

5. As accents, block print some bows in a random pattern within the cherry design area with danish blue glaze.

Fruit and Bows Apron, Oven Mitt, and Potholder

Pictured on pages 95 and 96.

GATHER THESE SUPPLIES

White chef's apron
White oven mitt
White potholder

Paint:
Colored glaze: bark brown,
    black cherry, bluebell,
    deep mauve, deep woods
    green, geranium red,
    ivy green, lemon yellow,
    and lilac

Tools:
Flat artists' brushes
Round artists' brush

Other Supplies:
Block printing designs:
    bows, fruits, and
    mixed berries

INSTRUCTIONS

Prepare:

1. Wash apron, oven mitt, and potholder to remove sizing. Dry and press.

Block Print the Design:

1. For tips, see "Block Printing on Fabric" on page 92.

2. Block print apron, oven mitt, and potholder using the following glaze colors: strawberries — geranium red; cherries — black cherry; small flowers — lilac; medium flowers — lemon yellow; raspberries — deep mauve;

leaves — deep woods green and ivy green; bows and ribbons — bluebell. Use the photo above as a guide for color and design placement.

3. Using a round artists' brush, paint the stems on the cherries with diluted bark brown glaze. Let cure for 24 hours.

Finish:

1. Heat-set paint with a dry iron.

Ivy Berry Kitchen

Pictured on page 97.

Designed by
Jane Gauss and Liza Glenn

The walls of this charming kitchen were block printed with trailing ivy vines and berries. Below the chair rail a green and white checked wallpaper was hung. The ivy vine motif was also block printed on a jelly cabinet, a wooden table, a bar stool, and a wall shelf.

An assortment of accessories, including wooden plates, canisters, and tea towels were block printed with fruits, berries, and leaves.

Ivy Berry Walls

Pictured on page 97.

GATHER THESE SUPPLIES

Paint:
Latex wall paint,
    flat finish: creamy white
Colored glaze: bark brown,
    black cherry, cranberry,
    deep woods green,
    ivy green, and sage green

Tools:
Flat artists' brushes
Round artists' brush

Other Supplies:
Block printing designs:
    ivy vine and mixed berries
Green and white
    checked wallpaper

INSTRUCTIONS

Prepare:

1. Prepare walls. See "Surface Preparation," pages 7-9.

2. Paint upper walls with creamy white latex wall paint. Let dry.

3. Paper lower walls with green and white checked wallpaper.

Block Print the Design:

1. Block print ivy leaves with deep woods green, ivy green, and sage green glaze, varying the colors. For a shaded effect, you can load the printing blocks with more than one color. Use the photo as a guide for color and design placement.

2. Block print the berries with black cherry and cranberry glaze. Place the berries among the vines at the top.

3. Using a round artists' brush, paint the vines with diluted bark brown glaze. Let dry for 24 hours.

Ivy Jelly Cabinet

Pictured on page 97.

GATHER THESE SUPPLIES

Wooden jelly cabinet

Paint:
Latex wall paint,
   flat finish: creamy white
Colored glaze: bark brown,
   deep woods green,
   ivy green, and sage green
Waterbase urethane varnish,
   satin finish

Tools:
Flat artists' brushes
Round artists' brush

Other Supplies:
Block printing designs:
   critters and ivy vine
Tack cloth
#0000 steel wool

INSTRUCTIONS

Prepare:

1. Prepare jelly cabinet. See "Surface Preparation," pages 7-9.

2. Paint jelly cabinet with two coats of creamy white latex wall paint. Let dry.

3. After the final coat has dried, rub the surface with #0000 steel wool. Remove dust with a tack cloth.

Block Print the Design:

1. Block print ivy leaves with deep woods green, ivy green, and sage green glaze. Apply one color at a time for each printing. Use the photo on page 97 as a guide for color and design placement.

2. Block print the inchworm at the bottom of the cabinet door with bark brown glaze.

3. Using a round artists' brush, paint the vines with diluted bark brown glaze. Let dry for 24 hours.

Finish:

1. Apply two coats of waterbase urethane varnish. Let dry.

Ivy Table

Pictured on pages 97 and 99.

GATHER THESE SUPPLIES

Wooden table

Paint:
Latex wall paint,
   flat finish: creamy white
Glazing medium: neutral
Colored glaze: bark brown,
   deep woods green,
   ivy green, and sage green
Waterbase urethane varnish,
   satin finish

Tools:
Rags or ragging mitt
Flat artists' brushes
Round artists' brush

Other Supplies:
Block printing design:
   ivy vine
Tack cloth
#0000 steel wool
Matte spray sealer

INSTRUCTIONS

Prepare:

1. Prepare table. See "Surface Preparation," pages 7-9.

2. Paint table with two coats of creamy white latex wall paint. Let dry.

3. After the final coat has dried, rub the surface with #0000 steel wool. Remove dust with a tack cloth.

Ragging the Table Top:

1. Mix one half part ivy green glaze with two parts glazing medium and one part water.

2. Rag table top. Let dry.

3. Using a flat artists' brush, paint around edge of table with two coats of ivy green glaze.

Block Print the Design:

1. Block print ivy leaves with deep woods green, ivy green, and sage green glaze. Apply one color at a time for each printing. Dark leaves are older growth leaves while the lightest ones are new leaves. Use the photo on page 99 as a guide for color and design placement.

2. Using a round artists' brush, paint the vines with diluted bark brown glaze. Let dry for 24 hours.

Finish:

1. Spray with two coats of matte sealer.

2. Apply two coats of waterbase urethane varnish. Let dry.

Ivy Bar Stool

Pictured on page 97.

GATHER THESE SUPPLIES

Wooden bar stool

Paint:
Latex wall paint,
   flat finish: creamy white
Wood stain: brown
Colored glaze: bark brown,
   deep woods green,
   ivy green, and sage green
Waterbase urethane varnish,
   satin finish

Tools:
Flat artists' brushes
Round artists' brush

Other Supplies:
Block printing design: ivy vine

INSTRUCTIONS

Prepare:

1. Prepare stool. See "Surface Preparation," pages 7-9.

2. Paint legs and rungs with two coats of creamy white latex wall paint. Let dry.

3. Stain seat with brown wood stain. Let dry.

Block Print the Design:

1. Block print ivy leaves with deep woods green, ivy green, and sage green glaze. Apply one color at a time for each printing. Use the photo on page 97 as a guide for color and design placement.

2. Using a round artists' brush, paint the vines with diluted bark brown glaze. Let dry for 24 hours.

Finish:

1. Apply two coats of waterbase urethane varnish. Let dry.

Ivy Shelf

Pictured on pages 97 and 100.

GATHER THESE SUPPLIES

Wooden wall shelf

Paint:
Latex wall paint,
   flat finish: creamy white
Colored glaze: bark brown,
   deep woods green,
   ivy green, and sage green
Waterbase urethane varnish,
   satin finish

Fruit Kitchen Accessories

Pictured on page 103.

Fruits, leaves, and flowers adorn this apron, hot pad, and appliance cover. Block printing is an easy, inexpensive way to add a custom decorator look to plain purchased kitchen accessories.

Berry Apron

Pictured on page 103.

Designed by
Kathi Malarchuk

GATHER THESE SUPPLIES

White apron with
  battenburg lace

Paint:
Colored glaze: burgundy,
  geranium red, ivy green,
  lemon yellow, and new
  leaf green

Tools:
Flat artists' brushes
Round artists' brush

Other Supplies:
Block printing design:
  mixed berries

INSTRUCTIONS

Prepare:

1. Wash apron to remove sizing. Dry and press.

Block Print the Design:

1. For tips, see "Block Printing on Fabric" on page 92.

2. Block print designs on the bib and on the lower edges of the apron using the following glaze colors: leaves with smooth edges — ivy green and new leaf green; large and small raspberries — burgundy and geranium red; rounded flower petals — lemon yellow shaded with geranium red. Use the photo on page 103 as a guide for color and design placement.

3. Use the handle end of a round artists' brush to add dots at the corners of the flowers with new leaf green glaze.

4. Using a round artists' brush, paint the stems and tendrils with diluted new leaf green glaze. Let cure for 24 hours.

Finish:

1. Heat-set paint with a dry iron.

Berry Hot Pad and Appliance Cover

Pictured on page 103.

Designed by
Kathi Malarchuk

GATHER THESE SUPPLIES

White hot pad
White cloth appliance cover

Paint:
Colored glaze: bark brown,
  black cherry, Christmas
  red, danish blue, ivy green,
  lemon yellow, and new
  leaf green

Tools:
Flat artists' brushes
Round artists' brush
Foam brushes, 1" (2)

Other Supplies:
Block printing design:
  fruits
White craft glue
Disappearing marker

INSTRUCTIONS

Prepare:

1. Wash hot pad and appliance cover to remove sizing. Dry and press.

2. Using excess printing block material from around the fruit designs, cut a $3/4$" square and a $1 1/4$" square.

3. Using white craft glue, glue one printing block square onto the end of the handle of each foam brush.

Block Print the Design onto the Hot Pad:

1. For tips, see "Block Printing on Fabric" on page 92.

2. Block print one $1 1/4$" square in each corner of the hot pad with danish blue glaze. Use the photo on page 103 as a guide for design placement.

3. Block print three $3/4$" squares on each side with lemon yellow glaze. Allow equal spacing between each square. Use the photo as a guide for design placement.

4. Block print the fruits and leaves with appropriate colors of glaze. Use the photo as a guide for color and design placement.

5. Using a round artists' brush, paint the stems with diluted bark brown glaze. Let cure for 24 hours.

Block Print the Design onto the Appliance Cover:

1. For tips, see "Block Printing on Fabric" on page 92.

2. To create the blue-checked border, use the disappearing marker and mark horizontal rows across the bottom, spaced approximately 1¼" apart. Make marks across the rows every 1¼". Starting at the lower left, block print a row of 1¼" squares with danish blue glaze. Repeat the procedure for second row. Position printing block so the lower left corner matches the upper right corner of the square on the first row. Repeat the procedure for third row. Use the photo on page 103 as a guide for design placement.

3. To create the yellow-checked border at the top of the cover, repeat the procedure for making blue-checked border. Use the ¾" squares with lemon yellow glaze. Use the photo as a guide for design placement.

4. Block print the fruits and leaves with appropriate colors of glaze. Use the photo as a guide for color and design placement.

5. Using a round artists' brush, paint the stems with diluted bark brown glaze.

6. Paint the tendrils with ivy green glaze. Let cure for 24 hours.

Finish:

1. Heat-set paint with a dry iron.

California-Style Dining Room

Pictured on page 105.

Designed by
Jane Gauss and Liza Glenn

In this dining room, walls are painted a warm, golden melon color. The chair rail, wainscoting, and wood trim are painted white. A block printed grape vine design trails along the wall corner.

On the floor is a faux rug that was painted, block printed, and stenciled.

Grape Vine Wall

Pictured on page 105.

GATHER THESE SUPPLIES

Paint:
Latex wall paint,
    flat finish: golden melon
Latex wall paint,
    semi-gloss finish: white
Colored glaze: bark brown, burgundy, deep purple, deep woods green, new leaf green, russet, and sage green

Tools:
Flat artists' brushes
Round artists' brush
Chalk or ¼" quilters' tape

Other Supplies:
Block printing design: grape vine

INSTRUCTIONS

Prepare:

1. Prepare walls. See "Surface Preparation," pages 7-9.

2. Paint walls with golden melon latex wall paint. Let dry.

3. Paint trim with white latex wall paint. Let dry.

4. Using chalk or ¼" quilters' tape, mark in the flow of the vine in the areas to be block printed.

Block Print the Design:

1. Block print the large leaves with deep woods green, new leaf green, and sage green glaze. Use the photo on page 105 as a guide for color and design placement.

2. Block print the smaller leaves to fill out the foliage with the same shades of green glaze. Interchange the leaf blocks to balance the design. Make certain to leave plenty of room for robust clusters of grapes.

3. Block print the grapes with various combinations of burgundy, deep purple, and russet glaze.

4. If necessary, add more leaves to fill out the design.

5. Using a round artists' brush, paint the grape vines with diluted bark brown and deep woods green glaze. Let the colors mix on the brush as you pull and twist it for a natural, gnarled vine look.

Trompe L'oeil Faux Rug

Pictured on page 107.

Designed by
Jane Gauss and Liza Glenn

This "rug" was painted directly on the hardwood floor. The stenciled fringe gives a trompe l'oeil look of elegance and whimsy. The rug's paint colors were custom mixed to match the colors of the chair fabric.

GATHER THESE SUPPLIES

Paint:
Latex wall paint,
    flat finish: dark green,
    dark red, and light cream
Colored glaze: bark brown,
    burgundy, deep purple,
    deep woods green, new
    leaf green, russet, and
    sage green
Wood sealer
Waterbase sealer/primer
Waterbase urethane varnish,
    satin finish

Tools:
Stencil brushes, 1" (3)
Ruler
Chalk pencil
Craft knife

Other Supplies:
Block printing design:
    grape vine
Border stencil: fringe or
    stencil blank material
Masking tape, 1" and 1½"

INSTRUCTIONS

Prepare:

1.   Prepare raw wood floors by sealing with a wood sealer made for raw wood. Apply to a clean, dry surface according to manufacturer's directions. When dry, you can walk on the wood in stocking feet.

2.   Prepare previously finished wood floors by removing all the wax and lightly sanding the surface. The wood does not need to be stripped.

3.   Using a chalk pencil, mark the center of the rug area. In this room, the center was determined by the location of the chandelier. An outside dimension for the faux rug was established based on the size of the table with the chairs around it.

4.   From the center, measure out in all directions half the length and half the width of the rug area. The finished size of this rug, minus the fringe, is 84" x 120". From the center, 60" was measured to each end and 42" to each side.

5.   Using a chalk line, mark diagonally from corner to corner, intersecting at the center point.

6.   Using 1" masking tape, tape along the outer edge of the rug area.

7.   Paint inside the tape area with a waterbase sealer/ primer. This primer coat will keep the paint from pulling off the surface. Let dry.

Paint the Rug:

1.   Paint the rug area with light cream latex wall paint. Let dry for at least 24 hours.

2.   Tape off and paint the dark green and dark red borders.

Use the photo on page 107 as a guide for color and design placement.

3.   Tape off and paint the ¼" and 3/16" dark green stripes around the center section.

Paint the Center Cross-Hatched Lattice:

1.   See "Painting Cross-Hatched Stripes" on page 93.

2.   Using 1½" masking tape, tape off diagonal stripes in the center rectangle. Tape and paint one diagonal at a time with the dark green border color. Start at one corner and work across to the other diagonal corner. Let dry.

3.   Repeat the procedure and paint the perpendicular stripes with the same color. Let dry.

Prepare a Paper Proof:

1.   Cut a piece of paper the width of the outside stripe. Block print some grape clusters. Let dry.

2.   Periodically step back and look at the project as you work. Aim for an open, scattered effect — not a regimented border. The amount of block printing is minimal so it does not detract from the impact of the rug or the wall accents. Do not clutter the area. You can always go back and add a pale, partial leaf or a hint of a vine in sparse areas.

3.   Cut out the patterns and lay them on the surface. Adjust to your satisfaction.

Block Print the Rug:

1.   Block print the leaves with deep woods green, new leaf

green, and sage green glaze. Use the paper proof as a guide for color and design placement.

2. Block print the grapes with various combinations of burgundy, deep purple, and russet glaze.

Stencil the Fringe:

1. For this rug, 4" fringe was used. Use a border fringe stencil or hand-cut a design of your own using stencil blank material and a craft knife.

2. Stencil the fringe with a combination of burgundy,

deep purple, and russet glaze. Use a different 1" stencil brush for each color of glaze.

Finish:

1. Apply three coats of waterbase urethane varnish. Let dry.

Block Printed Chest of Drawers

Pictured on page 109.

Designed by
Susan Goans Driggers

This old chest was revived with a pickling wash and then block printed.

Although pickling wash is usually used on raw wood, a pickled finish can be applied, with just a little more work, to any old pieces of furniture.

The bunny drawer pulls add a delightful, whimsical touch.

GATHER THESE SUPPLIES

Chest of drawers

Paint:
Pickling wash
Furniture stripper bleach
Latex wall paint,
    flat finish: light beige
Colored glaze: bark brown,
    ivy green, new gold leaf,
    and new leaf green

Tools:
Cellulose sponge
Flat artists' brush
Round artists' brush
Drill

Other Supplies:
Block printing design:
    ivy vine
Decorative drawer pulls (6)
Chalk
Wood filler
Matte spray sealer

INSTRUCTIONS

Prepare:

1. Remove drawer pulls. Fill holes with wood filler.

2. Prepare chest of drawers. See "Surface Preparation," pages 7-9.

3. If the wood is dark, bleach it with a furniture stripper bleach. If the bleaching doesn't lighten the wood enough, paint the chest with two or three coats of light beige latex wall paint. Let dry.

Pickle the Chest of Drawers:

1. Apply the pickling wash. If you painted the chest, this will be a faux pickled finish because you can't see the wood grain under the paint.

2. To intensify the pickling in the carvings and crevices, apply two or three coats of pickling wash to them with a brush.

Block Print the Design:

1. Using chalk, lightly draw the vines on the chest. Use the photo on page 109 as a guide for design placement.

2. Block print the leaves with ivy green and new leaf green glaze. Make some leaves only one color. When using both shades of green, load the colors in different places on the block each time for natural variation.

3. Using a round artists' brush, paint the vines with diluted bark brown glaze. Add tendrils and leaf stems with diluted ivy green glaze.

Shade the Block Printed Design:

1. Mix one part new gold leaf glaze to one part water. Load the leaf block and press it down almost on top of the leaf, offsetting the printing block just a bit to create a shadow. Use the photo below as a guide for color and design placement.

2. Use the same diluted glaze mixture to create shadows for vines, tendrils, and stems. Let dry.

Finish:

1. Spray with matte sealer.

2. Drill holes for the new decorative drawer pulls.

3. Install drawer pulls.

Block Printing on Wall Border Paper

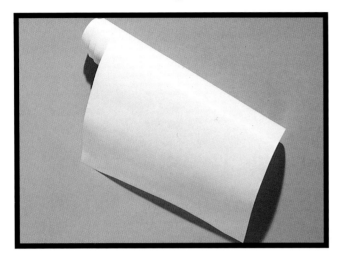

1 Wall border paper makes it easy to block print a border. You can block print the design on the paper and then hang the border on the wall. Blank wall border paper is especially helpful for those who want the greater convenience of block printing on a table surface or for beginners who are apprehensive about block printing directly on the wall.

2 Working on a flat surface, lay out three or four feet of border paper across a table so block printing can dry thoroughly before re-rolling. After block printing, allow the paint or colored glaze to cure at least 36 hours before applying border paper to the wall surface.

Trouble Shooting

- Keep a box of pull-up disposable wipes nearby when you are block printing. Use them to clean up paint from your hands or to repair the edge of a smudged print.

- If the first print is not complete:
  1. You have too little paint on the block. Apply more paint and reprint.
  2. You are not pressing around the outer edge of the block. Try "walking" your fingers around the block rather than pushing just in the center.

- If sliding is a consistent problem, try:
  1. Applying less paint.
  2. Not pressing with the heel of your hand; instead "walk" your fingers around the block.
  3. Blotting the block before printing on brown paper.

  4. Releasing the handle before pressing. You may be holding the handle and pressing at the same time.

- If you have a messy or smudged print:
  1. Make certain paint is not creeping up the handle.
  2. Remove a messy print with a disposable wipe or position the block over the same area and repeat the pressing technique.

- If veins in the block print are not clear:
  1. Thoroughly clean block to remove glaze buildup.
  2. Do not soak blocks for a prolonged period, they can become waterlogged.

- To store blocks, let them air dry. Store in the punch-out pad. This makes it easy to keep the shapes together within a set. Store in a plastic bag away from extreme heat or freezing cold.

Oak Leaf Entry Hall Wall Border

Pictured on page 111.

Designed by
Jane Gauss and Liza Glenn

For an elegant look, block print rustic oak leaves in gold to add a formal frieze to the tone-on-tone striped wallpaper in this entry hall.

GATHER THESE SUPPLIES

Paint:
Latex wall paint,
  flat finish: light cream
Glazing medium: neutral
Colored glaze: new gold leaf

Tools:
Sea sponge
Flat artists' brush

Other Supplies:
Block printing design:
  oak leaves
Blank wall border paper
Masking tape

INSTRUCTIONS

Prepare:

1. Paint wall border paper with light cream latex wall paint. Let dry.

Sponge the Background:

1. Mix one part new gold leaf glaze with three parts glazing medium.

2. Sponge entire surface of wall border paper with glaze mixture, lightly patting surface to create a very soft gold background.

Add the Striping:

1. Measure in ¾" from the top and bottom edges. Tape the outside lines. Measure and mark inward ¼" from taped lines. Tape outside second line, toward the middle of paper.

2. Paint between the taped lines with new gold leaf glaze. Remove tape. Let dry.

Block Print the Design:

1. Block print the leaves and acorns with new gold leaf glaze. Use the photo on page 111 as a guide for design placement. Let dry for 72 hours.

Spring Tulips Wall Border

Pictured on page 113.

Designed by
Kathi Malarchuk

These colorful spring tulips would brighten any room. The block printed wall border paper is hung above a chair rail.

GATHER THESE SUPPLIES

Paint:
Colored glaze: baby pink,
  bark brown, geranium red,
  ivy green, lemon yellow,
  new leaf green, sage
  green, and white

Tools:
Sea sponge
Flat artists' brush
Round artists' brush

Other Supplies:
Block printing design:
tulips
Blank wall border paper
Easy-mask painters' tape

INSTRUCTIONS

Sponge the Background:

1. Mix five parts white glaze with one part bark brown glaze. Add one drop of baby pink glaze. Mix with an equal amount of water.

2. Sponge entire surface of wall border paper with glaze mixture.

3. Mix one part ivy green glaze with remaining glaze mixture.

4. Lightly sponge wall border paper again. To soften the color, blot with a paper towel before glaze dries.

Add the Striping:

1. Using excess printing block material from the tulips printing block, cut a bar ⅜" wide the length of the block pad.

2. Block print the bar continuously with ivy green glaze to make the borders 1" from the top and bottom edges.

Block Print the Design:

1. Block print the tulips and leaves with appropriate colors of glaze. Make some tulips taller than others. Use the photo on page 113 as a guide for color and design placement.

2. Using a round artists' brush, paint the stems with diluted ivy green glaze. Let dry.

Cutting Your Own Printing Block

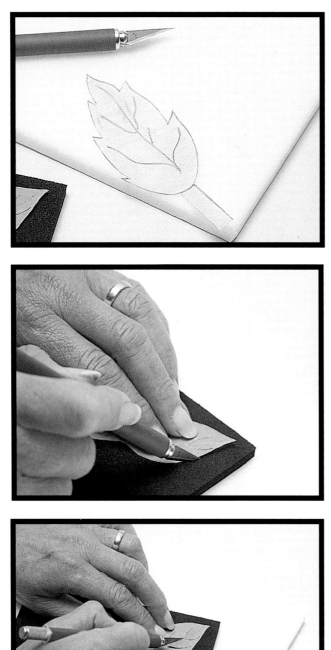

1 Choose a simple, silhouette type design. Trace the design with a sharp lead pencil onto tracing vellum. You can also use actual leaves or flowers by pressing them and placing them on a copy machine to reduce or enlarge as desired. Then trace the design onto tracing vellum. In either case, make certain you add a handle to the design.

To cut the outer edge, place the printing block material on glass. Place the pattern over the printing block material and secure it with tape. Use a very sharp craft knife to cut through the pattern into the pad.

2 On straight edges, make a clean, straight cut all the way through the pad. Keep the side of the blade flush against the pattern. Do not angle the blade. Achieve a straight up-and-down cut. On curved edges, use a sawing motion to cut about halfway through the pad. Then remove the pattern and use the cut lines as a guide to cut all the way through the pad. At points and turns, lift the blade and reposition it. Do not try to rotate the material with the blade in position.

3 To cut veins and details, hold the pattern to the surface and cut through the tracing. Cut halfway through the printing block material following detail markings. Be careful not to cut completely through the pad. Remove the tracing.

Test the block before working on your actual project. If there are ragged edges, put a new blade into your craft knife and carefully trim the ragged edges away.

Neoclassic Living Room

Pictured on page 117.

Designed by
Susan Goans Driggers

This warm, richly colored room has deep-tone colored glaze rubbed over the walls. A leaf design is block printed with bronze metallic glaze. The fireplace mantle has a ragged faux finish.

Glazed and Block Printed Walls

GATHER THESE SUPPLIES

Paint:
Latex wall paint,
   flat finish: white
Glazing medium: neutral
Colored glaze: geranium red,
   olde world bronze, and
   russet

Tools:
Sponge or sponging mitt
Flat artists' brush
Craft knife
Plumb line
Spirit level
Ruler and pencil

Other Supplies:
Printing block material
Sewing thread: any color
Tracing vellum
Masking tape

INSTRUCTIONS

Prepare:

1.   Prepare walls. See "Surface Preparation," pages 7-9.

2.   Paint walls with white latex wall paint. Let dry.

3.   Tape around molding and mantle to protect them from sponging.

Sponge the Walls:

1.   Mix one part geranium red glaze with six parts glazing medium. Add 1/4 part russet glaze.

2.   Sponge walls with glaze mixture. Use curved strokes to blend the color. You can rub any way in any direction. Reload the sponge or sponging mitt often to achieve a deep color on the wall surface. Work in sections about four feet wide.

3.   As the glaze dries, you can rub areas again until you get the color you want, but do not rub over any areas that aren't dry or you'll remove the glaze.

4.   Repeat the procedure until the walls are covered. Let dry. Remove tape.

Block Print the Design:

1.   Trace the leaf pattern onto tracing vellum. Cut out the leaf pattern from the printing block material.

2.   Measure the walls with a ruler along the width and height and mark evenly spaced lines 15-20" apart with a pencil (the distance depends on the size of the room — with a larger room or taller ceilings you can use the 20" measurement). Use a spirit level and a plumb line to make certain the lines are straight. Adjust the spacing so the block prints won't fall in the corners.

Another option would be to use sewing thread to connect the marks into a grid. This will allow you to see the placement of the block printed designs where the lines intersect.

3.   Block print the leaves at the grid intersections with olde world bronze glaze. Position the block the same way on the grid for each print and reload the block for each print to achieve a uniform pattern. Remove the thread. Let dry.

Ragged Fireplace Mantle

GATHER THESE SUPPLIES

Paint:
Latex wall paint,
   flat finish: white or cream
Glazing medium: neutral
Colored glaze: bark brown

Tools:
Rags or ragging mitt

Other Supplies:
Masking tape

INSTRUCTIONS

Prepare:

1.   Paint walls with white or cream latex wall paint. Let dry.

2.   Tape off walls around the mantle to protect it from ragging.

Rag the Mantle:

1.   Mix one part bark brown glaze with six parts glazing medium.

2.   Rag the mantle with glaze mixture. Remove tape. Let dry.

Tricks with Wallpaper

Wallpaper is a versatile covering for walls and furniture. Sometimes a patterned paper adds just the right touch, bringing design elements and colors together.

When you're ready for a change, a floral print can be antiqued with colored glaze. A simple stripe or geometric paper can be stenciled. You can also use wallpaper on furniture. Try cutouts for the look of hand painting or use as a covering for furniture or lamp shades.

The following pages show some wonderful tricks you can do with wallpaper to enhance your home decor.

Antiqued Wallpaper

Pictured on page 119.

Designed by
Susan Goans Driggers

Time paints its patina on surfaces, giving us a warm, grounded feeling when we are surrounded by it. We can hurry this process by adding an antique finish to wallpaper with a glazing mixture.

Flowered wallpaper done with this technique will have the look of a well-aged country bed and breakfast inn. The technique can also be used to tone down a too-bright paper or soften the tones of a high-contrast design.

GATHER THESE SUPPLIES

Wallpapered wall

Paint:
Glazing medium: neutral
Colored glaze: mushroom

Tools:
Sea sponge or sponging mitt

Other Supplies:
Masking tape

INSTRUCTIONS

Prepare:

1. To prepare existing wallpaper, make certain the wallpaper is clean and well-adhered to the wall. Repair as needed with paste or glue.

2. To prepare new wallpaper, make certain all excess adhesive has been wiped off.

3. Tape around molding to protect it from sponging.

Sponge the Wallpaper:

1. Mix mushroom glaze with glazing medium to make a light shade.

2. Sponge the glaze mixture over the wallpaper in a sweeping motion. This wall was worked using a vertical sweeping motion; vertical strokes were more attractive than horizontal or diagonal ones. Remove tape. Let dry.

Wallpapered Hope Chest

Pictured on page 120.

Designed by
Susan Goans Driggers

Embossed wallpaper applied to a plain chest adds a special touch. Covering a piece of unfinished furniture with wallpaper is a quick way to add texture and pattern.

The surface of the wallpaper is painted and glazed with color to emphasize the embossed texture of the paper.

GATHER THESE SUPPLIES

Unfinished chest with
  hinged lid

Paint:
Latex wall paint,
  flat finish: white
Glazing medium: neutral
Colored glaze: plum

Tools:
Sea sponge or sponging mitt
Craft knife

Other Supplies:
Embossed wallpaper
Matte spray sealer

INSTRUCTIONS

Prepare:

1. Paint the unfinished chest with one or two coats of white latex wall paint. Let dry.

Adhere the Wallpaper:

1. Adhere the embossed wallpaper to the sides and top of the chest. Leave the base area of chest and rim of lid uncovered. Trim edges with a craft knife.

2. Paint the entire surface, including the wallpaper, with another coat of white latex wall paint. Let dry.

Sponge the Wallpaper:

1. Mix plum glaze with glazing medium to desired shade.

2. Working one side at a time, sponge the glaze mixture into the textured design of the dimensional wallpaper.

3. Smooth the glaze over the exposed painted wood areas, then pat them with the sponge to create the mottled appearance. Complete all surfaces, rinsing the sponge as needed. Let dry.

Finish:

1. Spray with matte sealer.

Floral Wallpaper Accent Table

Pictured on page 121.

Designed by
Susan Goans Driggers

Wallpaper can be used to cover entire surfaces, and wallpaper cutouts can add interest to drawer fronts and table legs.

A coat of antiquing medium helps mellow everything and create the look of an aged hand painted table.

GATHER THESE SUPPLIES

Wooden accent table with
   drawer and tapered legs

Paint:
Latex wall paint,
   flat finish: creamy white
Antiquing medium:
   maroon and oak brown

Tools:
Cellulose sponge
Foam brush, 1"
Craft knife

Other Supplies:
Small print wallpaper,
   prepasted
Decoupage glue
Damp cloth
Matte spray sealer

INSTRUCTIONS

Prepare:

1. Prepare table. See "Surface Preparation," pages 7-9.

2. Paint table with two coats of creamy white latex wall paint. Let dry and sand between coats.

Adhere the Wallpaper:

1. Cut one piece of wallpaper slightly larger than the table top.

2. Adhere the wallpaper to the table top. If wallpaper is not prepasted, use decoupage glue to adhere it in place. Trim edges with a craft knife.

**Decorate the
Table Top and Legs:**

1. Cut out design motifs from the remaining wallpaper and adhere them to the drawer front, drawer pull, and to the lower part of the legs. Use the photo below as a guide for design placement.

2. If wallpaper glue remains on the surface, immediately wipe the residue away with a damp cloth. Let dry.

3. To create a smooth, uniform finish, apply a coat of decoupage glue to all surfaces of the table with a 1" foam brush.

Antique and Finish:

1. Using the 1" foam brush, apply a coat of maroon antiquing medium just to the edge of the table top and to the wooden buttons that cover the screws. Let dry.

2. Dampen the sponge and squeeze out excess water. Using the damp sponge, wipe a coat of oak brown antiquing medium on the entire surface of the table including the legs. Let dry.

3. Spray with matte sealer.

Stenciling on Wallpaper

If you'd like to stencil a room that is wallpapered, but are less than enthusiastic about the messy job of removing the paper, consider leaving the wallpaper in place and stenciling over it.

If the room is papered in a solid color, a tone-on-tone texture, or small print, stencil right over the pattern to add a decorator touch by blending stenciling with the wallpaper's color and design. Stenciling paint will adhere most effectively to flat finish papers. If you don't want to stencil directly on the wallpaper, stencil on blank wall border paper and apply it on top of the existing wallpaper.

If you are stenciling in an older home where the walls were papered to cover cracks in the plaster, there is no need to remove the paper before stenciling. Simply check to see that all seams are secure and reglue any loose sections. Paint the wallpaper with two or more coats of a flat- or satin-finish oil-based paint or a primer specifically designed to cover wallpaper. Let dry for 24 hours before stenciling.

Acrylic craft paint, dry brush paint, and paint crayons can be used to stencil on wallpaper. The stenciling should be light enough to let the background color and texture show through. Make certain the surface is free of dirt, dust, and grease.

Berries and Ivy Border

Pictured on page 123.

Designed by
Jane Gauss

Stenciling adds color to this room's monochromatic color scheme and enhances the striped wallpaper below the chair rail. Sponging adds additional color and texture to the upper walls.

GATHER THESE SUPPLIES

Wallpapered walls

Paint:
Latex wall paint,
   flat finish: white
Latex wall paint,
   semi-gloss finish: taupe
Glazing medium: neutral
Colored glaze: sage green
Dry brush paint: hunter green,
   truffles brown, vintage
   burgundy, and wild ivy
   green

Tools:
Sea sponge or sponging mitt
Stencil brush

Other Supplies:
Spot stencils: berries and ivy
   including flower pot
Border stencil:
   English ivy border
Lint-free terry cloth towel
4" x 6" index card

INSTRUCTIONS

Prepare:

1. Prepare upper walls.
See "Surface Preparation,"
pages 7-9.

2. Paint walls above chair
rail with white latex wall paint.
Let dry.

Sponge the Walls:

1. Mix sage green glaze with
glazing medium to make a
light shade.

2. Sponge the glaze mixture
on the white wall.

Paint the Chair Rail:

1. Paint the chair rail with

taupe latex wall paint to match the stripes in the wallpaper. Let dry.

Stencil the Border:

1. Using the berries and ivy spot stencil above the chair rail, connect the pots of ivy with trailing ivy that dips down below the chair rail. The English ivy border stencil is used to connect the motifs. Stencil some berries among the ivy leaves below the chair rail. Use the photo on page 123 as a guide for color and design placement.

2. Stencil the pots with truffles brown dry brush paint. Shade the rim with the curved edge of an index card.

3. Stencil the leaves, shading the outer edges and leaving the centers lighter, with a blended combination of hunter green and wild ivy green dry brush paint.

4. Stencil the berries with vintage burgundy dry brush paint. Let dry.

Product Sources

The products used to create the glazing, block printing, and stenciling can be found at many craft and do-it-yourself stores. Here is a listing of brand names used for the projects.

Decorator Products®

This group of products encompasses colored glazes, glazing medium, texturing mitts, and block printing designs.

• Decorator Blocks used for Block Printing:

Cut Your Own
Blank Block #53226

Wisteria Vine #53201

Ivy Vine #53202

Grape Vine #53203

Mixed Berries #53204

Fruit Assortment #53206

Bows #53224

Peaches and Pears #53207

Maple Leaves #53208

Oak Leaves #53209

Tulips #53213

Iris #53215

Lilac/Hydrangea #53217

Little Garden
Flowers #53219

Critters #53220

• Decorator Glazes®:

Used for block printing as well as mixing with neutral glazing medium for texturing walls.

Available in 2 oz. and 8 oz. sizes:

Neutral #53001

New Gold Leaf #53002

Silver Leaf #53003

Olde World Bronze #53004

Penny Copper #53005

White #53006

Lemon Yellow #53007

Sunflower #53008

Apricot #53009

Persimmon #5310

Russet #53011

Geranium Red #53012

Christmas Red #53013

Black Cherry #53014

Baby Pink #53015

Vibrant Pink #53016

Burgundy #53017

Deep Mauve #53018

Plum #53019

Deep Purple #53020

Pale Violet #53021

Lilac #53022

Blue Bell #53023

Danish Blue #53024

Nantucket Navy #53025

Sky Blue #52026

Soft Teal #53027

Sage Green #53028

New Leaf Green #53029

Christmas Green #53030

Ivy Green #53031

Deep Woods Green #53032

Bark Brown #53033

Black #53034

Linen White #53035

Warm Taupe #53036

Roseberry #53037

Pompeii Red #53038

Red #53039

Shrimp Bisque #53041

Tuscan Sunset #53042

Moss Green #53043

Alpine Green #53044

Italian Sage #53045

Malachite Green #53046

Patina #53047

Mushroom #53049

Russet Brown #53050

Neutral Wall
Glazing Medium,
48 oz. #53551

• Decorator Products® Tools:

Sponging Mitt #30105

Ragging Mitt #30106

Mopping Mitt #30107

Sea Sponging Mitt #30108

Spatter Tool #30121

French Brush #30122

Splashing Tool #30123

Multi Purpose
Comb #30124

Standard Comb #30125

Graduated Comb #30126

Natural Ocean
Sponge #30150

• Decorator Products® Accessories:

Brush Set #53453 contains one flat loading brush and one round veining brush

Product Sources

Blank Wall
Border Paper #53454

FolkArt Products®

• FolkArt® Acrylic Colors:

These are high quality brush-on acrylic paints. They are pre-mixed colors available in 170 color hues. Brushes cleanup with soap and water.

Available in 2 oz. squeeze bottles.

• FolkArt® Crackle Medium:

Available in
2 oz. size (#694),
4 oz. (#695),
and 8 oz. (#696)

• Finishes:

FolkArt® Waterbase Varnish #791

FolkArt Antiquing, available in 5 colors

FolkArt® Acrylic Sealer #788

Stencil Decor® Products

• Paints:

The following colors are available in Dry Brush Paints (first number listed) as well as Artist Paint Crayons (second number listed).

Cameo Peach
#26201, #26533

Turtle Dove Gray
#26202, #26534

Vintage Burgundy
#26203, #26535

Promenade Rose
#26204, #26536

Tea Time Rose
#26205, #26537

Truffles Brown
#26206, #26538

Ship's Fleet Navy
#26207, #26539

Herb Garden Green
#26208, #26540

Sherwood Forest
#26209, #26541

Wild Ivy Green
#26210, #26542

Ol' Pioneer Red
#26211, #26543

Cherries in the Snow
#26212, #26544

Romantic Rose
#26213, #26545

Blue Chintz
#26214, #26546

Wildflower Honey
#26214, #26547

Ecru Lace #26215, #26548

English Lavender
#26216, #26549

Sunny Brooke Yellow
#26218, #26550

White Linen
#26219, #26551

Dusty Rose
#26220, #26560

Bouquet Pink
#26221, #26561

Quilt Blue #26222, #26569

Vanity Teal #26223, #26570

Andiron Black
#26224, #26574

Eggplant #26225, #26580

Hunter Green
#26226, #26581

Maroon #26227, #26582

Indigo Blue
#26228, #26583

Sage Green
#26229, #26584

Periwinkle #26230, #26585

China Blue #26231, #26586

True Blue #26232, #26587

Liquid Acrylic Paint Sets available in
basic brights #26080,
country #26081, and
Victorian #26082

• Stencils:

Uncut Stencil
Blank #26667

Trellised Ivy #26611

Gardener's Ivy #26620

Ivy Cascade #26651

Eyelet Floral #26638

Magnolia Blossoms #26709

Beads and Bars Run
Stencil Tape #26421

Egg and Dart
Stencil Tape #26442

Bricks and
Cobblestone #26855

Garden Lattice #26851

Birdhouses #26853

Elegant Home™
Grape Vine #29001

Elegant Home™
Ivy #29002

Simply Stencils Decorator Background Hearts and Checks #28772

Lattice Collection #28776

Metric Conversion Chart

INCHES TO MILLIMETRES AND CENTIMETRES

INCHES	MM	CM	INCHES	CM	INCHES	CM
$1/8$	3	0.9	9	22.9	30	76.2
$1/4$	6	0.6	10	25.4	31	78.7
$3/8$	10	1.0	11	27.9	32	81.3
$1/2$	13	1.3	12	30.5	33	83.8
$5/8$	16	1.6	13	33.0	34	86.4
$3/4$	19	1.9	14	35.6	35	88.9
$7/8$	22	2.2	15	38.1	36	91.4
1	25	2.5	16	40.6	37	94.0
$1\,1/4$	32	3.2	17	43.2	38	96.5
$1\,1/2$	38	3.8	18	45.7	39	99.1
$1\,3/4$	44	4.4	19	48.3	40	101.6
2	51	5.1	20	50.8	41	104.1
$2\,1/2$	64	6.4	21	53.3	42	106.7
3	76	7.6	22	55.9	43	109.2
$3\,1/2$	89	8.9	23	58.4	44	111.8
4	102	10.2	24	61.0	45	114.3
$4\,1/2$	114	11.4	25	63.5	46	116.8
5	127	12.7	26	66.0	47	119.4
6	152	15.2	27	68.6	48	121.9
7	178	17.8	28	71.1	49	124.5
8	203	20.3	29	73.7	50	127.0

YARDS TO METRES

YARDS	METRES	YARDS	METRES	YARDS	METRES	YARDS	METRES	YARDS	METRES
$1/8$	0.11	$2\,1/8$	1.94	$4\,1/8$	3.77	$6\,1/8$	5.60	$8\,1/8$	7.43
$1/4$	0.23	$2\,1/4$	2.06	$4\,1/4$	3.89	$6\,1/4$	5.72	$8\,1/4$	7.54
$3/8$	0.34	$2\,3/8$	2.17	$4\,3/8$	4.00	$6\,3/8$	5.83	$8\,3/8$	7.66
$1/2$	0.46	$2\,1/2$	2.29	$4\,1/2$	4.11	$6\,1/2$	5.94	$8\,1/2$	7.77
$5/8$	0.57	$2\,5/8$	2.40	$4\,5/8$	4.23	$6\,5/8$	6.06	$8\,5/8$	7.89
$3/4$	0.69	$2\,3/4$	2.51	$4\,3/4$	4.34	$6\,3/4$	6.17	$8\,3/4$	8.00
$7/8$	0.80	$2\,7/8$	2.63	$4\,7/8$	4.46	$6\,7/8$	6.29	$8\,7/8$	8.12
1	0.91	3	2.74	5	4.57	7	6.40	9	8.23
$1\,1/8$	1.03	$3\,1/8$	2.86	$5\,1/8$	4.69	$7\,1/8$	6.52	$9\,1/8$	8.34
$1\,1/4$	1.14	$3\,1/4$	2.97	$5\,1/4$	4.80	$7\,1/4$	6.63	$9\,1/4$	8.46
$1\,3/8$	1.26	$3\,3/8$	3.09	$5\,3/8$	4.91	$7\,3/8$	6.74	$9\,3/8$	8.57
$1\,1/2$	1.37	$3\,1/2$	3.20	$5\,1/2$	5.03	$7\,1/2$	6.86	$9\,1/2$	8.69
$1\,5/8$	1.49	$3\,5/8$	3.31	$5\,5/8$	5.14	$7\,5/8$	6.97	$9\,5/8$	8.80
$1\,3/4$	1.60	$3\,3/4$	3.43	$5\,3/4$	5.26	$7\,3/4$	7.09	$9\,3/4$	8.92
$1\,7/8$	1.71	$3\,7/8$	3.54	$5\,7/8$	5.37	$7\,7/8$	7.20	$9\,7/8$	9.03
2	1.83	4	3.66	6	5.49	8	7.32	10	9.14

Index